A Spurious State of Confusion

By Charles M. Harper Sr.

A Spurious State of Confusion

By Charles M. Harper Sr.

Copyright © 2014 Guild Consultants, L.L.C. All rights reserved. No part of this work may be reproduced, stored in a retrieval system or transmitted, in any form or by any means, electronic, mechanical, photocopying, recording, or otherwise, in whole or in part, without the express written consent of the Author.

Printed in the United States of America

ISBN 978-1-312-36472-1

"Many persons are deluded by their vague suppositions that our mysteries are merely nominal; that the practices established among us are frivolous; and that our ceremonies might be adopted or waived at pleasure. O this false information, we have found them hurrying through all the degrees, without adverting to the propriety of one step they pursue, or possessing a single qualification requisite for advancement. Passing through the usual formalities, they have accepted offices, and assumed the government of Lodges, equally unacquainted with the rules of the institution they pretended to support, or the nature of the trust reposed in them. The consequences is obvious; whenever such practices have been allowed, anarchy and confusion have ensued, and the substance has been lost in the shadow."

- Thomas Smith Webb and James Fenton, Freemason's Monitor, 1865

Writers may express their opinions about the Fraternity, but their statements are not authoritative. Only Grand Lodges can make authoritative statements, and these apply only to their members. - Masonic Information Center, March 2001.

In these pages I express my opinions alone, developed through research and experience. In no way do they express or allude to the opinions of any Masonic Grand Lodge, Lodge or Masonic Body.

Table of Contents

Chapter 1

    Masonic Definitions..................................5

Chapter 2

    Spurious Freemasonry Reaching Epic Proportions in the United States....................................48

Chapter 3

    Prejudice and Discrimination Practiced in Freemasonry...95

Chapter 4

    An Extension of an Olive Branch: A Chance for Moral Progression....................................146

Chapter 5

    A Time to Display Moral Progression.............168

Chapter 6

    Tolerance: A True Measure of Compassion........179

Acknowledgements..192

About the Author...193

Bibliography...197

Chapter 1
Masonic Definitions

Before an exploration into the spurious state of confusion that exists within the masonic institution, which is primarily a problem for the Fraternity in the United States though it exists in other parts of the world, it is necessary to outline the long standing definition of words used within the masonic institution as they have sometimes different meanings in the context of masonic application. Many Masonic words are derived from their usage in the profane world, meaning outside of the construct of Freemasonry, and are altered or expanded upon to make them applicable to the institution's use. To place the use of these masonic words in their proper context throughout this book, it is necessary to explore their origins and the expansion of their use as the Fraternity has expanded in numbers and popularity around the globe.

The word clandestine will be explored from its initial profane use, and its transition of use into the Fraternity of Freemasons. From this word, using it as a foundation, we will explore its expanded use and the words necessary to describe what constitutes a Mason, Lodge, or Grand Lodge as regular, irregular, and finally, spurious. Finally, the confusion between what is considered regular, relative to the standard accepted definition set forth by the Commission on Information for Recognition of the

Conference of Grand Masters of North America, and the standard set forth by the United Grand Lodge of England, which is considered to be the Mother Grand Lodge of Speculative Freemasons of the world, and its relationship to the establishment of amity between two Masonic Grand Lodges, explored slightly in my previous book *Freemasonry in Black and White*, but will now be explored more in-depth.

The word clandestine, masonically, is similar to the public definition provided by the Penguin English Dictionary which states the meaning as: "to the held in or conducted with secrecy; surreptitious such as a clandestine meeting."[i] The etymology of the word is derived from the early French word clandestin, which is from the Latin word clandestinus, which came from the word clam, or secretly. The French word clandestin, from which it is derived, is defined by Boiste to be something fait en cachette et contre les lois, a phrase meaning in the French language, "Done in a hiding place and against the laws," which better suits the Masonic application which refers to what is not accepted, or is not authorized.[ii] People or organizations then, who operate outside of the confines or knowledge of accepted practices of society in various forms, are operating clandestinely. A simple example would be if one were to organize a business with a standard operating procedure and either an employee, or another entity altogether, operated under the guise of the original without its informed approval, or in secrecy, it is operating clandestinely.

The word clandestine, in the aspect of its definition including "not authorized," has allowed this word, prior to 1834, to be used as a description of the relationship between two sovereign grand lodges as communication or visitation is not authorized. Since the ritualistic application of the word is not explained during the Master Mason Degree, if one does not include the expanded attempts at the explanation of it over time by various authors, they must use this word in its application with the contractual relationship between a foreign grand lodge, and the grand lodge they have obliged to follow the laws, rules, and edicts. Therefore, any grand lodge that is not in amity with theirs, is thus clandestine regardless of whether they are regular in standing, according to the adopted landmarks of Freemasonry, or not. The Fraternity of Freemasons, noting each individual Grand Lodge is sovereign onto itself, has adopted certain rules or landmarks that are universally adhered too which makes them unified to a certain extent with a set standard of conformity which establishes a boundary between who and what are Freemasons, and who and what are not.

    Landmarks are a standard set of rules anciently composed that are applicable to the Masonic Fraternity, generated from the operatively formed lodges before 1599, and were made applicable for speculative masonic use in the continued tradition in the establishment of lodges and grand lodges, and the governing or standard operating procedure of the Craft. The first document demonstrating such ideas to later become landmarks was the Regius Poem or referred to as the Halliwell Manuscript, named after James O. Halliwell who was not a mason. It was estimated by Mr. Halliwell to have been written about 1390, or earlier.[iii] This poem gave direction on the treatment of an apprentice to his master, or teacher. It spoke of geometry and being charitable in the care of the distressed, and other such relatable matters that are found scattered throughout masonic traditions and teachings. These sentiments would stretch forth into the Constitutions of Edward III, the Regulations of 1663, 1703, 1717, 1720, and finally, the approved charges of 1722, presented into the first

Speculative Freemasons Grand Lodge in London, England by Dr. James Anderson and Dr. Jon Desaguliers. These Charges were:

1. Concerning God and Religion
2. Of the Civil Magistrate, Supreme, and Subordinate
3. Of Lodges
4. Of Masters, Wardens, Fellows, and Apprentices
5. Of the Management of the Craft in Working
6. Of Behavior

Following these six charges are the General Regulations of 1721 that are separated into 39 more different specific regulations of the Craft. It is important to note that even though each grand lodge is sovereign and decides for itself which ancient charges they will make their own, most stem from these original charges. The first six charges relate to behaviors of a Mason and management of the Craft. The additional general regulations are more specific to the organizational rules that are considered to be the ancient usages though now modernized, but are relatively the same. Let us explore some examples.

Rule VI. "But no man can be entered a Brother in any particular lodge, or admitted to be a member thereof, without the unanimous consent of all the members of that Lodge then present when the candidate is proposed, and their consent is formally asked by the master."[iv]

In modern times, this practice still exists as a petitioner must be balloted upon for acceptance into membership by the lodge and depending on the jurisdiction, either one or more votes can be casted to reject a candidate with no explanation being given. This protects each individual mason from being pressured to cast a vote one way or another by his Brethren, and strengthens the integrity of the ballot. It also, unfortunately, can be used unmasonically to control the lodge if just one member not balloting for the good of masonry, but just himself.

More relative to the point of the rules regarding what may constitute a lodge to be clandestine is a defiance to general regulation no. VIII, which states:

"No set or number of brethren shall withdraw or separate themselves from the lodge in which they were made Brethren, or were afterwards admitted members, unless the lodge becomes too numerous;

nor even then, without a dispensation from the Grand Master or his Deputy; and when they are thus separated, they must either immediately join themselves to such other lodge as they shall like best, with the unanimous consent of the lodge to which they go, or else they must obtain the Grand Master's Warrant to join in forming a new lodge."[v]

What this passage illustrates are rules as to the forming of a new lodge within a masonic jurisdiction. A regularly made Mason can leave their lodge to join another within their masonic jurisdiction, or in a foreign one where amity has been established that provides for acceptance of members from foreign constitutions by means of a compact, providing they are in good standing with the lodge that made them Masons. If numerous Masons desire to form a new Lodge, they may do so if given a warrant or dispensation to meet as a lodge by the Grand Master of the same jurisdiction in which they are already members. And in some cases, members can be included from foreign jurisdictions providing there is in amity compact that provides for such actions. If the Masons were to simply form a new lodge within the jurisdiction of the grand lodge to which they were previously beholding without a dispensation, this would be an irregular action and they would be forming a clandestine lodge, a lodge outside of the established system. In effect, they would have formed an irregular lodge. This lodge's members, existing as an irregular lodge, would not have the rights and benefits of masonic communication or travel to lodges as one within the system. If they offered to men masonic degrees and membership under the auspice that they are operating in the same manner as one with a dispensation or warrant, they would be acting fraudulently.

The word clandestine first appears masonically well after the birth of the first speculative Masonic Grand Lodge in the world, the Grand Lodge of England, having its first meeting in June of 1717 in London, England. It was not needed at the time as there were no rival Grand Lodges to threaten the sovereignty of the first established Grand Lodge. By 1713 in England, speculative lodges were all but defunct as they existed separately, not organized into any system at that point as it was not popular, or a sign of status yet, to be a Freemason. It would not become popular to even be a member of the Fraternity until Samuel Prichard's release of the expose *Masonry Dissected*. This would be the most popular exposure of the Mason's ritual, following two earlier prints of *A Mason's Examination*, and *The Flying Post or Postman*. The word clandestine had not appeared in any of these exposes as there were no rival grand lodges organized to challenge the original Grand Lodge's sovereignty.

The popularity of Freemasonry and rise of exclusionary practices, forbidding common Irish and Scottish stonemasons from acceptance into membership based upon their social status in society, and even some already initiated speculative freemasons traveling to England for work from joining the speculative Lodges, would cause the birth of a successfully formed rival Grand Lodge in England on July 17, 1751, the world's first successfully sustaining clandestine grand lodge of speculative Freemasons at that time. This Grand Lodge, dubbing themselves as the Ancients due to their practices of inclusion of the common working craftsman into their fold which was more in line with the precepts of the masonic institution, unlike the premier grand lodge which tended to cater to the aristocracy due to its popularity and appearance of societal status, was considered by the premier grand lodge to be formed irregularly. This denotes that it did not have permission to form a lodge or grand lodge from the premier grand lodge. In the minutes of the Old King's Arms Lodge, then no. 38, but now no. 28, a reception of a Mason from an unknown lodge who was "made in a clandestine manner in an unconstituted lodge and was made in the three degrees and paid what is customary." These "re-makings" of a mason by re-obligating them in the degrees of the Craft in a new masonic jurisdiction are similar to a practice that may be enacted on a case by case basis by Prince Hall Grand Lodges in the United States and internationally commonly known as "healings." Men presenting themselves as Masons are investigated for their general masonic knowledge, character, and are examined to be of good report. If found worthy of election to membership, they are obligated under the constitution in which they have sought, and they take their place amongst the membership of the lodge, entitled to all the rights and privileges therein. This was a masonic means to accept a man who had been made a mason in what was believed to be in an irregular form, and make them regular according to the practices of constitution they sought admittance.

As Masonic Grand Lodges began to grow steadily in popularity and expand across the globe, prior to the uniting of the rival grand lodges of England in 1813, the word clandestine was common terminology, but not ritual terminology. Neither the emulation, nor the standard ritual of Scottish Freemasonry possess this word in the obligation of a Master Mason. It came to be ritual terminology used mostly in the United States. Currently, most all regular Grand Lodges in the United States have the term of clandestine with the exception of a rare few. The question becomes why? If this term was used in the common description of rival Grand Lodges in England and the United States, how did it become included in the American ritual and not in other rituals?

> "The word 'clandestine' falls with unhappy significance upon modern Masonic ears, but it did not in those days mean quite the same thing as it does to Masons of this age, Prior to the 'Lodge of Reconciliation' and the formation of the United Grand Lodge of England in 1813, the two Grand Bodies of England, the 'Moderns' (who were the older) and the 'Antients' (who were the younger, schismatic body) each considered the other 'clandestine."[vi]

A note must be made here. According to John Belton, author of *The English Masonic Union of 1813: A Tale Antient and Modern*, who also cites Bernard E. Jones of *Freemasons Guide and Compendium* to further support his research, that according to the transactions of the Grand Committee of the Most Ancient and Honorable Fraternity of Free and Accepted Masons on February 5, 1752, Lodges no. 2-10 "being representatives of all the Ancient Masons in and adjacent to London" declared that Brother Laurence Dermott qualified and was then elected the Grand Secretary. He also states that there is "no evidence that any of the lodges belonging to the 1717 Grand Lodge actually left to create a new grand lodge."[vii]

To the point of rituals during this time, they were no more than poems, memorized by masons advancing through the masonic degrees in an effort to prove proficiency and did not contain the word clandestine. It must be stated that the memorization of these catechisms does not fully equip a man to truly understand the gateway of the transformative process introduced to him, but it is one of the minimum standards in which proficiency is demonstrated. The word clandestine would not appear in written ritual until after the Baltimore Convention of 1834, and not even in full written form for many United States Grand Lodges until the late 1900's as many used only cyphers. It is reasonable to conclude that the usage of the word clandestine in American Masonic Ritual was due to the culture of America, which to this day has a history that still arouses emotions of a horrid past that introduces verbal venom into many conversations about the amity between the Prince Hall Grand Lodges and the Grand Lodges of each state, and the lack thereof in the southern states of America between the two Grand Lodges. Cultural relativism can be used to explain this continuing lack of amity between these two existing regular grand lodges in the nine southern states of America and is a concern that will be explored further in this book.

> "Today the Masonic world is entirely agreed on what constitutes a clandestine body, or a clandestine Mason; the one is a Lodge or Grand Lodge unrecognized by other Grand Lodges, working without right, authority or legitimate descent; the other is a man "made a Mason" on such a clandestine body."[viii]

This statement may have been true in 1935, well after the end of the Joseph Cerneau episode of degree peddling in 1806[ix], and in relation to Prince Hall Masonry even though African-Americans could no longer be enslaved as of 1863. The gross misunderstanding of the application of the word Free-born would have been men believe that former slaves not born free and the descendants of slaves, could not be made masons. Unfortunately, this is still a common belief in 2014. However in the context of the time, the word was used relative to its understanding during the period. However, the population of spurious masonic grand lodges that sprang to life in the early 1900's with the actions of the infamously expelled Freemason John G. Jones, who was expelled from the Most Worshipful Prince Hall Grand Lodge of Illinois for contumacy, and have grown to epidemic proportions since, calls for a reevaluation of the use of this word.

These fraudulent organizations have been continually on the rise since 1904, perpetuated by a culturally isolated practice of fraternal brotherhood within the United States. Mutual recognition beginning in 1989 between the Grand Lodges of the United States and the Prince Hall Grand Lodges should have stemmed the tide of growth for these spurious organizations, but without regular widespread visibility of the interactions and the lack of establishing the bonds of brotherhood on the subordinate lodge level between the jurisdictions sharing state territories, room for prejudicial manipulation and spin simply perpetuated a unyielding cultural separation that has still not reached a plateau. For this reason, it is time to revert back to the earlier understanding of what clandestine meant masonically, before it became a 'bad word.'

    The word Clandestine needs to be simply defined, once again, as the absence of an amity compact between to existing grand lodges, or stated more commonly- two grand lodges without recognition of one another, irrelevant to their determination of their regularity. The word clandestine need not be an adjective describing a grand lodge, but simply a word that plainly defines the relationship between two sovereign grand lodges who have organized in compliance with the widely accepted standards laid down by James Anderson, which were accepted by the first speculative masonic grand lodge in the world, the Grand Lodge of England. While all grand lodges are sovereign and it rests in their determination as to who they enter into amity agreements with, it is without contention that the influence of the Anderson's Constitutions play an integral role in how a grand lodge defines regularity in those they examine seeking amity. When it needs to be determined why two grand lodges are clandestine to one another, explanations using more terminology are then applicable. This brings us to the next significant words of this chapter to be used throughout this book- regular, irregular, and spurious.

The word regular is defined by the *American Heritage Dictionary of the English Language* as customary, usual, or normal.[x] Hence, regularity means symmetry or regular occurrence, a process either repeated continually in the same manner or in the same standard. Though speculative freemasonry in a lodge setting occurred long before the organizing of the first grand lodge in England, there was a repeated manner, some regularity of how gentleman were initiated into a speculative lodge. Even after the organizing of this grand lodge, Bernard E. Jones states in *Freemasons Guide and Compendium* that the grand lodges were more of a "rallying point," rather than a regulator of the ritual performed in the various lodges being chartered by it. As the popularity expanded and more lodges either transitioned from trade guilds or organized specifically as speculative masonic lodges, a need of conformity ensued to ensure that all being made masons were done so in a similar fashion.

In 1723, the Grand Lodge of England required that all men initiated into their respective lodges within the craft not be made Master Masons in their lodges, but only at the Grand Lodge. This lasted for 10 years until the edict was repealed. However, it does make sense that an organization would desire that all men made Masters under their jurisdiction would be done so in a manner that was consistent with all other lodges under its authority. This is in modern times a form of branding a product.

Any organization offering an original product would have any reproduction of its product produced in strict conformity with the original design to ensure the integrity of the product. The Fraternity of Freemasons also had to ensure the integrity of the institution by ensuring that all lodges subordinate to the Grand Lodge of England at the time were making masons in the usual customary standard. This standard done repeatedly established regularity, or a regular way of making masons. Any Lodge of speculative Freemasons being desirous of representing the same "brand" had to abide by the same standard operating procedures, the same regular way of making masons, which means they had to adhere to regularity. With the standard firmly established, any lodges forming or making masons outside of the organizational structure of the Grand Lodge, would be irregular. To further establish this understanding of terminology usage, any person made a mason, any lodge or grand lodge organized outside of the established rules, or otherwise known as the ancient usages, in any manner or form not acceptable by the original source of establishment, must be considered irregular, or not regular.

In the continental United States, there exists 94 Grand Lodges that are defined as regular by the Conference of Grand Masters of North America, and the Conference of Grand Masters Prince Hall Masons, Inc. First here listed are the "mainstream" Grand Lodges, followed by the Prince Hall Grand Lodges:

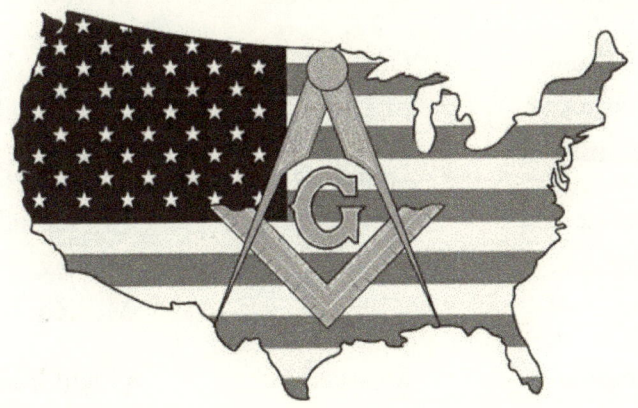

Grand Lodge of Alabama

Grand Lodge of Alaska

Grand Lodge of Arizona

Grand Lodge of Arkansas

Grand Lodge of California

Grand Lodge of Colorado

Grand Lodge of Connecticut

Grand Lodge of Delaware

Grand Lodge of District of Columbia

Grand Lodge of Florida

Grand Lodge of Georgia

Grand Lodge of Hawaii

Grand Lodge of Idaho

Grand Lodge of Illinois

Grand Lodge of Indiana

Grand Lodge of Iowa

Grand Lodge of Kansas

Grand Lodge of Kentucky

Grand Lodge of Louisiana

Grand Lodge of Maine

Grand Lodge of Maryland

Grand Lodge of Massachusetts

Grand Lodge of Michigan

Grand Lodge of Minnesota

Grand Lodge of Mississippi

Grand Lodge of Missouri

Grand Lodge of Montana

Grand Lodge of Nebraska

Grand Lodge of Nevada

Grand Lodge of New Hampshire

Grand Lodge of New Jersey

Grand Lodge of New Mexico

Grand Lodge of New York

Grand Lodge of North Carolina

Grand Lodge of North Dakota

Grand Lodge of Ohio

Grand Lodge of Oklahoma

Grand Lodge of Oregon

Grand Lodge of Pennsylvania

Grand Lodge of Puerto Rico

Grand Lodge of Rhode Island

Grand Lodge of South Carolina

Grand Lodge of South Dakota

Grand Lodge of Tennessee

Grand Lodge of Texas

Grand Lodge of Utah

Grand Lodge of Vermont

Grand Lodge of Virginia

Grand Lodge of Washington

Grand Lodge of West Virginia

Grand Lodge of Wisconsin

Grand Lodge of Wyoming

Prince Hall Grand Lodges within the United States, and their jurisdictions[xi]

- Grand Lodge of Alabama
- Grand Lodge of Alaska
- Grand Lodge of Arizona
- Grand Lodge of Arkansas
- Grand Lodge of California
- Grand Lodge of Colorado
- Grand Lodge of Connecticut
- Grand Lodge of Delaware
- Grand Lodge of District of Columbia
- Grand Lodge of Florida
- Georgia Grand Lodge of Georgia
- Grand Lodge of Hawaii
- Grand Lodge of Illinois
- Grand Lodge of Indiana
- Grand Lodge of Iowa
- Grand Lodge of Kansas
- Grand Lodge of Kentucky
- Grand Lodge of Liberia
- Grand Lodge of Louisiana
- Grand Lodge of Maryland
- Grand Lodge of Massachusetts
- Grand Lodge of Michigan
- Grand Lodge of Minnesota
- Grand Lodge of Mississippi

Grand Lodge of Missouri	Grand Lodge of Ohio	Grand Lodge of Utah
Grand Lodge of Nebraska	Grand Lodge of Oklahoma	Grand Lodge of Washington
Grand Lodge of Nevada	Grand Lodge of Oregon	Grand Lodge of West Virginia
Grand Lodge of New Jersey	Grand Lodge of Pennsylvania	Grand Lodge of Wisconsin
Grand Lodge of New Mexico	Grand Lodge of Rhode Island	Grand Lodge of Wyoming
Grand Lodge of New York	Grand Lodge of South Carolina	Grand Lodge of Virginia
Grand Lodge of North Carolina	Grand Lodge of Tennessee	

All the 94 Grand Lodges listed here are deemed regular Grand Lodges within the United States. There are over 450 more spurious grand lodges, a list that grows monthly, now existing within the borders of the United States. These spurious organizations deem themselves regular as well. As each grand lodge decides for itself its standard of regularity and whom they deem as regular, only the Grand Lodges listed are recognized as adhering to the standards of regularity established by the United Grand Lodge of England, and by both the Conference of Grand Masters of North America, and the Conference of Grand Masters Prince Hall Masons, Inc. Recognition, or amity, established between many of these grand lodges is only possible by the standards of regularity to which they all adhere. Whether the choice is made to establish amity or not, it has no bearing on the proving of a grand lodge as regular.

The Conference of Grand Masters of North America's Recognition Commission, formed in 1952 and which all Grand Lodges of the United States holds membership in except the Grand Lodge of West Virginia, provides data for use by the United States Grand Lodges, and "does not attempt to influence or recommend what action should be taken. The Commission serves in an investigative and advisory capacity only."[xii] The standards of Recognition are summarized as follows:

1. Legitimacy of Origin

2. Exclusive Territorial Jurisdiction, except by mutual consent and/or treaty.

3. Adherence to the Ancient Landmarks – specifically, a Belief in God, the Volume of Sacred Law as an indispensable part of the Furniture of the Lodge, and the prohibition of the discussion of politics and religion.

The Phylaxis Society, the very credible research society for the Prince Hall Grand Lodges equivalent in an academic standard to the Philalethes Society, also noted the common standards regarding regularity.

1. Regular in its origin

2. Independent and self-governing

3. Adhere to 'landmarks'

From the report of the Phylaxis Society:

REGULARITY OF ORIGIN

The original Grand Lodges (England, Ireland and Scotland) were formed by private Lodges which had formed themselves Time immemorial Lodges, in English parlance. The 18th Century, three State Grand Lodges in the United States of America were formed by two Lodges, and one was formed by a Grand Convention of Masons Subsequent Grand Lodges follow the modern rule in paragraph 4.

A Grand Lodge must have been established by: a) a recognized Grand Lodge, or b) three (nowadays) or more regularly constituted private Lodges, formed in accordance within the rules and customs of a regular Grand Lodge.

A Grand Lodge must have undisputed authority over Craft (or basic) Freemasonry within its jurisdiction, and not be subject in any way to or share power with any other Masonic body.[xiii]

United Grand Lodge of England

BASIC PRINCIPLES FOR GRAND LODGE RECOGNITION

Accepted by the Grand Lodge, September 4, 1929

The M.W. The Grand Master having expressed a desire that the Board would draw up a statement of the Basic Principles on which this Grand Lodge could be invited to recognize any Grand Lodge applying for recognition by the English Jurisdiction, the Board of General Purposes has gladly complied. The result, as follows, has been approved by the Grand Master and it will form the basis of a questionnaire to be forwarded in future to each Jurisdiction requesting English recognition. The Board desires that not only such bodies but the Brethren generally throughout the Grand Master's Jurisdiction shall be fully informed as to those Basic Principles of Freemasonry for which the Grand Lodge of England has stood throughout its history

1.   Regularity of origin; i.e. each Grand Lodge shall have been established lawfully by a duly recognized Grand Lodge or by three or more regularly constituted Lodges.

2.   That a belief in the G.A.O.T.U. and His revealed will shall be an essential qualification for membership.

3. That all Initiates shall take their Obligation on or in full view of the open Volume of the Sacred Law, by which is meant the revelation from above which

is binding on the conscience of the particular individual who is being initiated.

4. That the membership of the Grand Lodge and individual Lodges shall be composed exclusively of men; and that each Grand Lodge shall have no Masonic intercourse of any kind with mixed Lodges or bodies which admit women to membership.

5. That the Grand Lodge shall have sovereign jurisdiction over the Lodges under its control; i.e. that it shall be a responsible, independent, self-governing organization, with sole and undisputed authority over the Craft or Symbolic Degrees (Entered Apprentice, Fellow Craft, and Master Mason) within its Jurisdiction; and shall not in any way be subject to, or divide such authority with, a Supreme Council or other Power claiming any control or supervision over those degrees.

6. That the three Great Lights of Freemasonry (namely, the Volume of the Sacred Law, the Square, and the Compasses) shall always be exhibited when the Grand Lodge or its subordinate Lodges are at work, the chief of these being the Volume of the Sacred Law.

7. That the discussion of religion and politics within the Lodge shall be strictly prohibited.

8. That the principles of the Antient Landmarks, customs, and usages of the Craft shall be strictly observed.[xiv]

As can be noticed by an examination of all three, there is uniformity in the standards. If one were so inclined to review the standards of regularity held by all the grand lodges listed as regular in the United States, which includes all the Prince Hall Grand Lodges, the same standards will exist. It is the strict adherence to these standards that are examined when one grand lodge seeks to establish amity with another grand lodge. The International Free and Accepted Modern Masons, a spurious group, as well as new grand lodges referring to themselves as "regular," have applied for a recommendation to the COGMNA recognition Committee. They were denied. "A great many /"Grand Lodges"/ continue to appear in North America each year which do not meet the standards for recognition. Further, most of these Grand Lodges make no effort to achieve regularity or even establish a relationship with the regular Grand Lodges into whose jurisdiction they have inserted themselves."[xv]

The one glaring exception is the Exclusive Territorial Doctrine, which is an American enforced rule that is a double-edged sword that states that no grand lodge can be organized or exist in an established territory where a previous grand lodge has established territorial jurisdiction as being the first in the territory. Outside of the United States, Grand Lodges have jurisdiction over its lodges. Within the country, Grand Lodges exercise jurisdiction over a territory.

"Grand Lodges in the United States have adhered to State lines as the limits of their activities, but this has not been so strictly the custom elsewhere."[xvi]

As an example of the reinforcement of the state boundaries within the United States being the jurisdictional boundaries rather than simply over lodges comes from the 57th Annual Communication of the Grand Lodge of Louisiana where the Grand Master communicates to the Craft that the Grand Orient of France had established amity with a spurious Masonic body by the name of Supreme Council of the Sovereign and Independent State of Louisiana. In his address, he declared that amity would be resolved calling this body both "spurious and clandestine body," meaning it was a fraudulent body and without amity with the Grand Lodge of Louisiana.

> "It will become your painful duty to take notice of this action of the Grand Orient of France, and make such decree as in your wisdom may be found expedient and necessary, to sustain the dignity of this Grand Lodge and maintain its authority over Craft Masonry in this Jurisdiction. There can be no divided authority. Upon one principle we are all agreed, and while we have life we will sustain it. The Grand Lodge of Louisiana will never submit to a divided jurisdiction, and in this position she will be sustained by every Grand Lodge in North America, for all are interested alike in sustaining each other. This principle once abandoned, the power of Masonry for good is gone. Discord and confusion will reign supreme, and the sun of Masonry will set in a sea of darkness."[xvii]

This doctrine is useful when being applied to actual spurious, meaning fraudulent, grand lodges attempting to invade and establish itself where a regularly organized Grand Lodge existed first, and/or where one such as a Prince Hall Grand Lodge has been established and has entered in a mutual agreement to share the territory. As we will explore later in this book in regards to the lack of amity between the southern Grand Lodges of the United States and the Prince Hall Grand Lodges, the sharp edge of this doctrine can be presumed to be applied in an unmasonic manner unfortunately, and it contributes to the existence and growth of spurious Grand Lodges in the south and the isolated onus placed upon the Prince Hall Grand Lodges to combat them. As we have defined what is considered regular standards and adversely the irregular standards, actions not residing within the scope of regularity, the definition of spurious and how it relates to Freemasonry will now be explained.

Spurious is defined as "Lacking authenticity or validity in essence or origin; not genuine" by the American Heritage Dictionary of the English Language, and from the Late Latin spurius, from Latin, illegitimate, probably of Etruscan origin. What defines a mason as a spurious mason, a lodge, or grand lodge as spurious? By the definition of spurious being something that is not valid or genuine, a spurious mason is one who was victimized by an organization presenting itself to the individual as being a legal Masonic organization, legal being stated in the context of the ancient customs adopted by every regular and well governed Grand Lodge of Masons, and according to codes of law in several states of America, actually civilly illegal. Is victimized the proper word for those who become members unsuspectingly of spurious organizations presenting themselves as traditional Freemasons? When they first join the answer is "yes." When a spurious Lodge presents itself as a traditional lodge, this references the means by which the lodge or grand lodge represents itself to the public that they offer the same membership as the likes of George Washington, Benjamin Franklin, Thurgood Marshall, Kweisi Mfume, and many others were affiliated with, which is not true.

Many spurious lodges and grand lodges use the faces of well-known masons in the advertisements of their lodges on websites and Facebook pages, as well as other social media outlets, in an attempt to legitimize themselves in the eyes of the public. These organizations have no famous members to attract a non-mason to join so they must use famous Prince Hall Masons if they are predominately Black themselves. Here is an example of a spurious lodge presenting itself as a traditionally regular lodge:

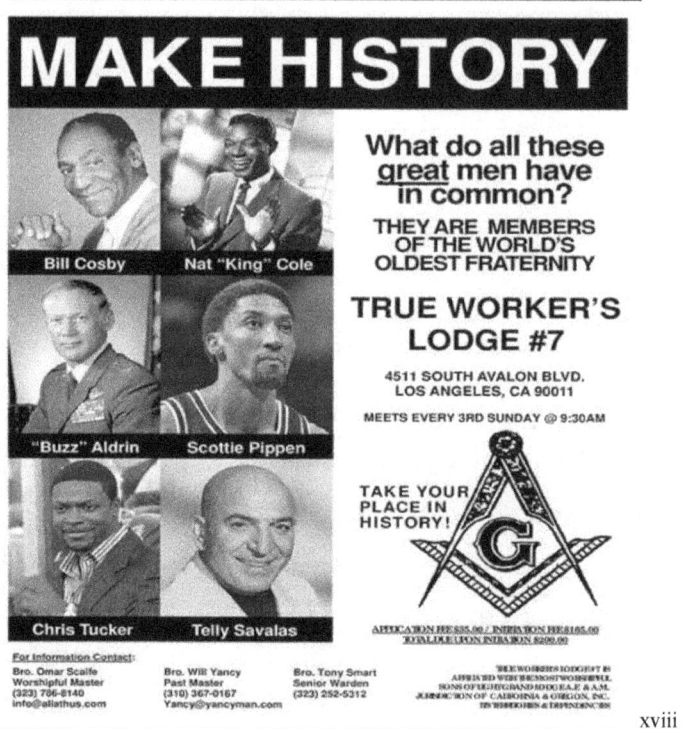

True Worker's Lodge No. 7, subordinate to The Most Worshipful Sons of Light Grand Lodge Ancient Free and Accepted Masons Jurisdiction of California and Oregon, Inc., whose history states, "The Most Worshipful Sons of Light Grand Lodge A.F. & A.M. Jurisdiction of California was organized and founded on April 10, 1943 at 652 Fourth Street, San Francisco, CA in the New Washington Hotel. Rev. Joseph S. Pough was the President of the organization," was never organized by lodges regularly formed and chartered by existing regularly organized grand lodges having lineage to the Grand Lodge of England, Ireland, Scotland, which England had amity with both before 1813, or the Grand Orient of France before it changed its landmarks designating it as irregular. The history explains the lodges coming together to form this grand lodge stating:

> After instituting three Lodges; Sons of Light #444 (being granted a Charter from the Most Worshipful United Grand Lodge of the State Florida); Rising Star Lodge #412 (being granted a Charter from the Most Worshipful King David Grand Lodge State of Mississippi); and Orange Grove Lodge #138 (being granted a Charter from the Most Worshipful King Solomon Grand Lodge District of Columbia); Rev. Joseph Samuell Pough (Grand Master); Rev. F.B. Banks (Deputy Grand Master); Walter Bennett (Grand Senior Warden); Charles Herman Ward (Grand Junior Warden); J.L. Pugh (Grand Secretary); and Duffy Robinson (Grand Treasurer) established and incorporated the Most Worshipful Sons of Light Grand Lodge A.F. & A.M. Jurisdiction of California on October 21, 1943.

None of the Grand Lodges listed as having chartered these lodges in California were regularly organized either. At first glance, it would appear that this organization followed the rules and they may have believed they had, but not in their entirety as the Prince Hall Grand Lodge or the Grand Lodge of California had in their forming. Members will cite that they adhered to the rule of having a grand lodge organized by three or more lodges, but they fail to follow the other rule of having legitimate origins.

To the ad and how spurious lodges attract members, the ad asks what do all the people in the photos have in common, answering they were all members of the Fraternity of Freemasons. Chris Tucker, the famous comedian from movies such as *Rush Hour* and *Friday*, is not a Mason listed in any regular Grand Lodge. The other men are all Prince Hall Masons or mainstream Masons. This is a clear example of fraud being practiced. This fraud and the results of it will be explored later in this book. This lodge is attracting men under the auspice that if they become members there, they will be Freemasons just like the famous men shown. However, men made masons in spurious lodges will never be able to enter these lodges where the celebrities were made masons.

Spurious Lodges and Grand Lodges believe themselves formed according to ancient standards, which were more definitively outlined after the Baltimore Convention. The more modern standard of forming a grand lodge is having three or more lodges come together which are chartered from a competent jurisdiction, and whose members must be in good financial standing, and establish themselves in a territory where no other Grand Lodge exists. Before the Convention, grand lodges were formed sometimes by a convention, as was the case with the Grand Lodge of New Jersey, or formed with a lodge chartering other lodges as was the case with African Lodge No. 459 in Massachusetts, and Mother Kilwinning Lodge No. 0 in Scotland. African Lodge was chartered by the Grand Lodge of England on September 20, 1784 and Kilwinning Lodge was a Time Immemorial Lodge, a Lodge that existed before the Grand Lodge system was formed to govern speculative Freemasonry. Taken out of the context of the era, men use these examples as justification to organization lodges and grand lodges now where grand lodges have already been established for more than 150 – 250 years.

The process is repeated to no end and is used as justification for a masonically legal existence and are unfortunately incredibly routine.

The routine that is often used and presented publically are foreign to most regularly made masons. For example: a spurious lodge that may have been in existence for one month to even 60 years, subordinate to a spurious grand lodge and who gains incorporation from the state they reside in as a 501c3 nonprofit, and even uses exposes such as *Duncan's Ritual and Monitor* by Malcolm Duncan, *Lester's Look to the East* by Ralph P. Lester, or even *More Light* written by H.W. Sander, designs their own charters, and open themselves for business.

This patent of this process belongs to John G. Jones, pictured, an expelled mason from Illinois in 1903.

According to Right Worshipful Brother Daryl Andrews, author of *Masonic Abolitionists: Freemasonry and the Underground Railroad in Illinois, Personification of Hope: A Legacy of National African American Political Leadership*, as well as other historical books, wrote in the Fall 2012 Prince Hall Masonic Journal, referencing the 1887 and 1903 Most Worshipful Prince Hall Grand Lodge of Illinois proceedings, that both Jones and his brother Theodore Wellington Jones were initial suspended by Grand Master Joseph W. Moore. Jones was initially suspended for issuing Grand Lodge communications without permission. The brothers then called for a Masonic Convention without the approval of the Grand Master. After attempting to file a lawsuit against the Grand Lodge, the lawsuit was dropped and the brothers were restored to active membership. J.G. Jones was eventually expelled in 1903 by Grand Master Henry Burris.[xix]

John G. Jones manipulated the story of his visit to visiting Luxemburg and presented through a letter he wrote, that he had obtained a charter to establish Masonic Grand Lodges in the United States. Hon. D. Antoine Lilly,

M.P.S., Appointed Officer of the Commission on Bogus Masonic Practices of the Phylaxis Society presented an explanation entitled, "We are NOT all Brothers: An Introduction to Clandestine Masonry." In this presentation to the 2014 Phylaxis Convention, he explains the beginnings of what would become the spurious legacy of the once honorable mason, John G. Jones. Lilly explains that the General Grand Masonic Congress received its charter rite August 1847, which is simply an article of incorporation, in Washington D.C. It was revised in 1870 and reorganized by John G. Jones in Cleveland, Ohio on the date of August 9, 1889 under the name of National Masonic Congress A.F. &A.M. He notes that this Congress of Grand Lodges was reportedly established in Chicago in 1877.[xx] This practice of believing that incorporating a business in the name of a Masonic Grand Lodge replaces the need to be regularly established by three or more regularly chartered lodges in a territory has become the norm of spurious masonic organizations. The attitude is that if John G. Jones did it and no one stopped him, then it is okay.

This epidemic is greatly more abundant in the African-American community due to numerous reasons we will explore in this book, but it is not limited to the African-American Community.

It must be noted that this book is not directed towards Co-Masons or Feminine Masonic disciplines. Though these disciplines are clandestine due to irregular standards of the inclusion of woman, which traditional Freemasonry does not, there have been woman Freemasons dating back to the 1700's in England where Elizabeth St. Leger is reported to have been caught eavesdropping on an Irish Masonic lodge of her fathers while it was tiled, and was initiated into the Craft. Another famous woman in the feminine discipline made a mason was Maria Deraismes. Taken from the History of Woman's Freemasonry:

> "In 1892, the Lodge Les Libres-Penseurs in Le Pecq initiated Maria Deraismes, a well-known feminist writer and activist. This was against the rules of the Grand Orient which closed the Lodge. Maria Deraisme remained a close friend of Georges Martin who persuaded her to create a Lodge where both men and women could work in full equality. She gathered a small number of women and a few Freemasons, and in 1893, created the Droit Humain (DH), a Masonic organization open to both men and

women, which eventually spread to all continents, including in the United States where it is known as Co-Masonry."[xxi]

An announcement in the 'Grand Lodge News' of the United Grand Lodge of England that followed the March 10, 1999 Quarterly Communication of UGLE:

"There exist in England and Wales at least two Grand Lodges solely for women. Except that these bodies admit women, they are, so far as can be ascertained, otherwise regular in their practice (emphasis added!). There is also one which admits both men and women to membership. They are not recognized by this Grand Lodge and intervisitation may not take place. There are, however, informal discussions from time to time with the women's Grand Lodges on matters of mutual concern. Brethren are therefore free to explain to non-Masons, if asked, that Freemasonry is not confined to men (even though this Grand Lodge does not itself admit women). Further information about these bodies may be obtained by writing to the Grand Secretary."

"The Board is also aware that there exist other bodies not directly imitative of pure antient Masonry, but which by implication introduce Freemasonry, such as the Order of the Eastern Star. Membership of such bodies, attendance at their meetings or participation in their ceremonies is incompatible with membership of this Grand Lodge."[xxii]

Thus, the feminine disciplines though irregular, and are thus clandestine to traditional Freemasonry, do have origins found within the Masonic Fraternity definitively from the Grand Orient of France's requirement their existence would be attached to a traditional all male masonic lodge. This history provides evidence that these orders are simply irregular, not spurious.

Chapter 2
Spurious Freemasonry Reaching Epic Proportions in the United States

It has not gone unnoticed, the emergence of enthusiasm for masonic education. It is not that this excitement has not existed before, but in the past several years, it has started to become more widespread. The masons responsible are both known, and unknown, all of which desire no fame or glory, but simply that their contributions improve understanding and advance the greatness of our institution. It is all filling a need made realized by a return to what the Craft historically has represented, and what it meant to be observant to the traditional practices of Freemasonry.

As the tides turn, and the purpose of our institution returns ever so slowly to its roots, we are all a witness to a reverse in a trend similar to when Laurence Dermott saw the decline in focus of the first Grand Lodge of England towards the goal of Freemasonry, and assisted in organizing the Grand Lodge of England affectionately known as the "Ancients," due to their self-proclaimed adherence to the ancient usages of the Craft. Today, just as in yesteryear, a return to the founding principles will effectively serve to properly educate our brethren and assist in the perpetuation of the order. However, just as the culture of the first grand lodge changed from making good men better to appeasing the aristocracy, effectively placing their heads in the sand, so too has the coattails of success of the last membership explosion in 1959 allowed us to place our heads in the sand for way too long once again. The lack of insightful and applicable masonic education, which has undermined our continued growth and success, has also allowed the embers of spurious Freemasonry to grow.

According to the book, *American Freemasons* by Brother Mark Tabbert, since the days of "Joseph Cerneau and his followers sold Scottish Rite degrees to anyone willing to pay for them, …African-American entrepreneurs created dozens of clandestine Masonic grand lodges for black men that competed with Prince Hall Freemasonry."[xxiii] This is corroborated by David Gray's book, *Inside Prince Hall*, where Gray lists almost 200 irregular Grand Lodges in the United States. This book, written in 2004, has a low listed number compared to now in 2014, just 10 years later. The count by both Paul Bessel's website that lists all grand lodges regardless of classification and the Phylaxis society division of Bogus Masonry led by Antoine Lilly in Kansas, places the number well over approximately 400 combined. Some clandestine, or more specifically classified spurious masonic grand lodges, are more well-known than others and more readily spotted than others. They may receive warrants or charters from other previous existing spurious Grand Lodges, giving them the belief that they have followed the landmarks of the Craft which collectively states that for a lodge to be regular, it must be chartered by an existing regularly formed Grand Lodge. Well if a man does not know what constitutes a regular grand lodge or lodge in the first place, you have a residual failure in understanding repeating itself multiple times.

The gentleman organizing these spurious lodges most often were never made masons in a regular lodge, or they were made masons and expelled, or in other cases, have never set foot in a lodge of masons however they may be defined. The General Masonic Congress organized by expelled mason John G. Jones in the early 1900's, mentioned in Chapter one and well explained in the book *History of the Shrine* by Joseph A. Walkes Jr., has spawned many numerous factions. There is the International Modern Free and Accepted Masons formed by William Banks, an attorney, in 1950, Banks being a former member of the Modern Free and Accepted Masons. It has never been shown that Banks was ever made a mason, much less an expelled one. The IFAMM's were incorporated by

Banks on January 2, 1959 in Dover, Delaware, Maryland. In the original documents, it can be seen that the original incorporation was for a beauty hair school, but this description as marked out and the name of the organization was placed as the name to be incorporated.

In Chicago alone, the spurious Grand Lodges existing are near totaling 70 according to Prince Hall Mason Carlton Smith and Adrian Cooley of Illinois and members of the Phylaxis Society which is a masonic society that does an excellent job of masonic education, and has a division that specifically tracks the forming of spurious grand lodges.

Charting the number of spurious masonic grand lodges are easier as they file taxes being state registered charitable organizations claiming nonprofit tax status. As they file taxes and these records are public record, one can gain a count of their existence. There is a new influx of spurious grand lodges forming in the United States, and perhaps one that may grow quicker than the rest. They are grand lodges warranted by the Masonic High Council, which is subordinate to the Regular Grand Lodge of England.

To immediately remove any confusion, the Regular Grand Lodge of England is NOT the United Grand Lodge of England, which is regular in its formation and existence and which all traditional Freemasonry derives its standards of regularity and legitimacy of origin, with the exception of the Grand Lodge of Louisiana which, according to Michael R. Poll of the 16th District of the Grand Lodge, has a unique existence in America and derives its origin from French Freemasonry. The Grand Lodge of Louisiana is still in amity with the United Grand Lodge of England. No, this Regular Grand Lodge of England was organized in 2005 by Rui Gabirro, an expelled Mason.

According to Brother Edward King, who owns and operates the website Masonicinfo.com, "On December 14, 2005, Rui L. Gabirro of Brethren in Amity Lodge #8650 under the United Grand Lodge of England was expelled from Freemasonry."[xxiv] Rui Gabirro appears to have been expelled for the same action as John G. Jones, a Mason from the Prince Hall Grand Lodge of Illinois. According to an article written by Brother Ezekiel M. Bey of the Phylaxis Society, "John G. Jones and William Gray were charged, tried, and expelled from all the rights, benefits and privileges of Masonry for gross unmasonic conduct,

October 14, 1903. Their false statements relating to a "split in the Grand Lodge of Illinois," and their fraudulent scheme of pretending to confer legally the degrees of Masonry from the first to the thirty-third degree exposed."[xxv] Here is a photo of Rui Gabirro taken from Masonic High Council the Mother High Council of the World Facebook page, a popular social media cite that attempts to give credibility to spurious organizations.[xxvi]

On January 25, 2005, the Masonic High Council, the Mother High Council of Ancient and Honorable Fraternity of Free and Accepted Masons was formed and then established the Regular Grand Lodge of England in London on the 5th of March, 2005. According to the newsletter published April 2005 by the Regular Grand Lodge of England on February 25, 2005, Mr. Rui Gabirro of the Mother High Council, was elected as Secretary General of the Masonic High Council for England and Wales. He was expelled by the United Grand Lodge of England on December of the same year. Joining a spurious masonic organization that is not in amity with one's own, and then forming a grand lodge irregularly, all while he was a member of the United Grand Lodge of England is not permitted and is gross unmasonic conduct. In both situations, it displays contumacy.

The Masonic High Council on their public website states:

> "Special Notice to MHC Masons and Masons in Amity with the Masonic High Council the Mother High Council concerning the existence of some Irregular and Unrecognized Grand Lodges.
>
> The Masonic High Council the Mother High Council reminds all Members of the Craft that they should take great care before joining any organization which purports to be Masonic. If in

doubt a written enquiry should be made of the Secretary General. There are some self-styled Masonic bodies that do not meet these standards, e.g. which do not require a belief in a Supreme Being, or which allow or encourage their members to participate as such in political matters and some of these self-styled Masonic bodies have even become Service Clubs. These bodies are recognized by the MHC the Mother High Council as being Masonically irregular, and Masonic contact with them should be avoided at all times."[xxvii]

It is interesting that an irregularly formed masonic organization would echo the sentiments of the oldest Grand Lodge in the world in the standards of regularity, yet violates them in its organizing. Yes, it is for the purpose of fraud in the pursuit of making men who do not know what regularity is feel comfortable about joining. Here is a statement issued by the United Grand Lodge of England in regards to the Regular Grand Lodge of England:

> It is being claimed that the formation of the "Regular Grand Lodge of England" is a result of a major schism within the United Grand Lodge of England that has led to a significant number of

Lodges and individual members withdrawing from the United Grand Lodge of England. Those claims are malicious lies, with no foundation in reality. Of the known members of this new spurious and fraudulent body, only two appear to have had any connection with regular Freemasonry in England. Rather than Lodges having defected to it, there appears to be only one active Lodge, self-constituted this year. Their website link shows links to other irregular, self-constituted Grand Lodges in India and Europe, including the Grand Lodge of France, who's Grand Chancellor, Michael Singer, has been appointed representative of the "Regular Grand Lodge of England" for France.[xxviii]

Here is what is unfortunate. This practice of forming Grand Lodges by expelled Masons, men who were never made masons in a regular Lodge, or by the departure of a mason or lodge from an already spurious formed Grand Lodge, is unfortunately common place in the United States. As stated, today there exists more than 400 spurious grand lodges in the United States and all formed irregularly. Many times these are predominately African-American organizations, though there orders such as the

1613 Nation in existence, led by the now infamous Brad Cofield. As such, mostly Prince Hall Freemasons are left to confront their masonically illegitimate existence by themselves. When confronting spurious masons and attempting to educate them about regularity and more specifically, legitimacy of origin, well, most Masons outside of Prince Hall Masons are relatively oblivious to the problem, or why spurious masonry is a problem.

Many more spurious Grand Lodges, originally warranted by the Regular Grand Lodge of England, have surfaced in recent years who are affiliated with, and received their warrant from the Masonic High Council, and the Regular Grand Lodge of England. As of 2014, these grand lodges exist in Illinois, Florida, North Carolina, Indiana, Nevada, Virginia, Georgia, Missouri, and it is anyone's guess how many more will have been formed by the time one reads this book. The majority of the spurious Grand Lodges in the United States are predominately African-American in membership. This is due to America's dark past of slavery and fight for civil rights which has created an emotional distrust of information presented by white Americans, or Prince Hall Masons, as they are viewed as having to have run to the "white man" for permission to be masons by way of recognition.

Though African-American men have been made regular Freemasons since before 1717 as with Brother John Pine in England, and in the United States with Prince Hall in 1775, the golden age of fraternalism brought with it the manipulation of a lack of amity between the Prince Hall Grand Lodges and mainstream Grand Lodges for centuries, a problem continually resolved with amity being establish between these grand lodges in each territory. Official reasons are not forthcoming from these remaining southern Grand Lodges as to why there has been no amity yet established. Conversations often had concerning the relationships amongst white members of the fraternity often range from confusion as to which African-American Grand Lodge is the legitimate grand lodge, a refusal to allow whites to sit in lodges with African-Americans as during the long period of segregation Blacks could not sit in lodges anyway, and simply failed attempts thus far in a few of the states for varies reasons. With 40 of the states having at the minimum of mutual recognition, even with two without having visitation, it leaves an awfully big black eye on American Freemasonry and questions by the public yet to be answered officially.

Rui Gabirro, listed as Bro. Rui Alexander Gabirro, Secretary General, Masonic High Council for England and Wales, 16 Victoria Park, Dover, Kent, CT16 1QS ENGLAND in the April 2005 Regular Grand Lodge of England Newsletter No. 1, appears in several photos in Virginia in 2010, and is mentioned by Carlton S. Brigham, the Grand Master of the Regular Grand Lodge of Maryland, as being a very nice fellow and a part of the organizing of the Regular Grand Lodges in America. He has mobilized his members to take advantage of the seemingly epidemic outbreak of spurious grand lodges in the United States, which has had exponential growth in the last 10 years due to information about freemasonry now readily given on the internet and the public not knowing any difference between authentic and spurious.

I had a conversation via Google Hangout, which was recorded, in which I interviewed the current Grand Master of the Regular Grand Lodge of Maryland, Carlton S. Brigham. To ease the Masons reading this regarding the speaking to a clandestine mason and the masonic obligation I have taken, I am obliged not to converse upon the secrets of the Craft which include the signs, passes, grips, and masonic ritual. I began the conversation explaining such before we proceeded, and I recorded the conversation. I must note that Carlton Brigham was very forthcoming, cordial, and professional during the interview. He presented himself as genuine about his beliefs and pursuits. This is not unusual though. There are thousands of spurious masons who are very good men, and who believe they are legitimate masons in every sense of the word. As my questions were asked though, his answers were the customary response of a person who seemed to be a good man, but also a spurious Mason.

This is the history presented by Mr. Brigham about the origins of his Grand Lodge. He stated he traveled to "France in 2006 and received a warrant from the Regular Grand Lodge of England to become a Grand Lodge, and began working as a Grand Lodge under the constitution of the Masonic High Council of the United States." He received his warrant in a ceremony located "downtown," at the Grand Lodge of France. The Masonic High Council of the United States, now defunct, included the Regular Grand Lodge of Virginia, Illinois, California, New Jersey, and North Carolina. He was a Past Grand Master of the

Regular Grand Lodge of Virginia. As to Rui Gabirro, he heard that he was expelled, but he saw no proof. He was shown by Mr. Gabirro proof of membership with the United Grand Lodge of England, and also a demit from the same Grand Lodge. As noted earlier, Mr. Gabirro was expelled from the United Grand Lodge of England and therefore any demit would have been fraudulent.

Mr. Brigham's Grand Lodge now operates under a council by the name of the United Masonic Assembly of the United States of America. This assembly includes the Regular Grand Lodge of Maryland, Illinois, Texas, New Jersey, and Georgia.

He states they are practicing the "Ancient Accepted Rite Freemasonry, not Scottish Rite." When I asked how he felt about invading the territory of the Grand Lodges already existing, he said they are "performing a totally different Rite, and therefore, to his understanding, there is no problem." He stated his Rite practiced is from the "time of the Moderns and Ancients of 1717." It was clear that though Mr. Brigham was passionate about doing the work of Freemasonry, he clearly did not have an understanding of what derives masonic regularity, which determines if a masonic grand lodge is even eligible for recognition to another regularly established Grand Lodge.

Some may question as to the harm of the existence of these spurious Grand Lodges. Let us look at a recent example. Claims on social media have been made by ever growing confident and outspoken members such as Darius Anderson of St. Louis, Missouri, a member of the Regular Grand Lodge of Missouri who received its warrant, as Mr. Anderson states, from the United Masonic Assembly of the United States of America, which all derived from Mr. Brigham's original visit to obtain a warrant from the Regular Grand Lodge of England. He states that Prince Hall Affiliated members, and members of mainstream Freemasonry, are starting to make visitations and becoming members of this organization as they are impressed with their regularity. Said by, Darius Anderson, on a social media page February 9, 2014:

"The RGLM had a nice, productive meeting last night. I brought two PH Masons to see our productivity. By the time we were done, they were thanking me for introducing them to something real! (Their words, not mines) They were shown our lineage & was impressed. Please keep in mind that these brothers were traveling since the early 70's. They are great men & it showed through their character!" He went on to say: "Steven Hale, Charles M. Harper Sr., and Everett Allen Sayre Jr. Our Templars are out of the Vatican in Rome! Where do yours come from, the cereal box?! Lmao. 1307 it is now 2014. Just 50 years ago masonry was condemned in most parts of Europe. It is now 2014, & Grand Lodges are being erected once again. Learn something." This is the same gentleman who took advantage of a gracious offer and was invited to a joint event in Missouri between the Most Worship Prince Hall Grand Lodge of Missouri, and the Grand Lodge of Missouri.

Prince Hall Master Mason Steven Hale in response to him:

"This is the exact type of shady behavior that causes me to believe the negative about out Darius Anderson. For a couple of years now you have been throwing MWGM Michael Johnson under the bus for extending to you visitation to a district raising (under the pretense that you and your entire lodge were going to healed under the MWPHGL of Missouri). You have used its occurrence for nothing but your own egotistical gain.....and now you are doing the same again with supposed two men who you say were active PH Masons that visited your new group and were so thoroughly in "awe" of it that they immediately denounced their former lodges and begged for membership in your group under your leadership. But their names and PH lodges are to be kept a secret at their request....but you're free to post its occurrence????"

To dispel any misrepresentation made by Darius Anderson of his attendance at this joint event, a statement was made by the then, Deputy Grand Master of the Most Worshipful Prince Hall Grand Lodge of Missouri, Michael Trent Johnson, "Darius Anderson and another elder member of St. Matthews were invited to talk with our PHA brothers further about possible community work in the future. Yes, this was on the night of my Lodge's regular meeting, but upon their arrival, we went into round table mode in our ballroom. No open bible, alter, etc. we sat at 6 ft. tables and had what I thought was a healthy discussion on community service projects and proposals for the same. However, this effort never panned out either." He also went on further to state that he "Explained the process of "healing of non-PH masons into our ranks as PHA Masons. Darius Anderson seemed quite interested in that possibility, but requested more time to think about it."

This is the unmasonic attitude being taught displayed to the public and by unknowing men, instructed by the inadequate education of seemingly good men such as spurious mason Carlton Brigham. While the actions of Mr. Anderson appear sullied, he is actually a victim of predatory spurious masonic organizations. His remarks and actions are actually rather typical and are repeated multiple times a day, thousands of times a year in the dark world of spurious Freemasonry where supreme presidents of more than 30 masonic grand lodges such as Illustrious James O. Dogan, 33°who, according to tax forms filed for the year 2011, earned a portion of the more than $400,000.00 a year. The organization has a Board of Directors and he, as the governing person to it as their website states, the "International Free & Accepted Modern Masons, Inc. and Order of Eastern Star extends from coast to coast; from the Great Lakes to the Gulf of Mexico, on the Bahamas Islands and Alaska, is the president.

There are more than 3,500 lodges and chapters with a membership of approximately 400,000 families represented. In addition, our youth courts consists of over 2,000 members."[xxix]

James O. Dogan[xxx]

Men and woman are physically beaten, humiliated, fraudulently taken advantage of for large sums of money in these organizations, all to obtain what they believe are the rights and privileges of a regular Freemason in the United States. They are victimized every day by what I believe is a spurious masonic epidemic. There are over 70 spurious Grand Lodges in Illinois, over 200 in New York and more than 103 in California, and large clusters in many other major cities around the United States. A full listing of spurious Grand Lodges can be found courtesy of the Phylaxis Society at:
www.thephylaxis.org/bogus/bogusgrandlodges.php. This listing was last updated in 2006. It has grown exponentially even since this time. Another listing can be found at www.masonicinfo.com.

To substantiate the claims of physical abuse at the hands of spurious organizations such as James Dogan's and numerous others, former members have come forth with their stories to now share them with the public in hopes of preventing more men seeking the Fraternity of Freemasons to be drawn into these spurious groups as victims.

Carlton Smith, a former member of the International Modern Free and Accepted Masons organization who is now a member of the Prince Hall Grand Lodge of Illinois, suffered a permanent injury to his arm in the year 2000, sustained from receiving the Mark Master degree in the Royal Arch Chapter of the William V Banks Grand Lodge, a grand lodge subordinate to the International Free and Accepted Modern Masons, while he was tied down with ropes.

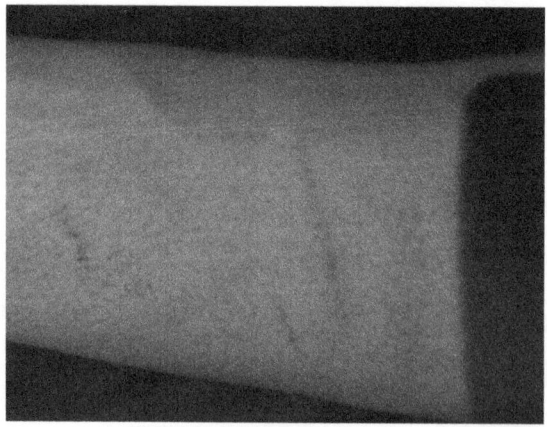

The Mark Master Degree of the Royal Arch is one of the Capitular Degrees. It teaches a man to discharge his several duties punctually and with precision, the duty of assisting a distressed brother is illustrated in a symbolic manner. Historically the degree illustrates the process by which the work on the temple accomplished by each craftsman was identified.[xxxi] The ritual of this degree does not instruct in any manner of from that any form of physical or mental hazing is to be conducted on the candidate in any capacity. Having gone through and participated in the degree myself as a member of Lafayette Chapter no. 2, subordinate Chapter to the Grand Royal Arch Chapter of the State of Illinois, there is nowhere in the performing of this ritual that one could presume to tie a candidate down with ropes - Nowhere.

The next photo is of Carlton Smith's knee. It was burned, leaving a permanent injury during a Shriner initiation in 2002 with the same grand lodge, after he stumbled on crackling sand, spread on the top of an electric griddle, which was placed on the floor. The sand was baked in an oven at 450°F for five hours before the initiation into the International Free and Accepted Modern Masons Shriners subordinate grand lodge, William V Banks Grand Lodge. Prior to cross the incredibly hot sand laid upon an electric griddle, he was doused with water. Other horrific stories have been shared as well by men who are now members of Prince Hall Grand Lodges, and did not know that hazing is not permitted in regularly practiced Freemasonry.

In the photo, the William V. Banks Grand Lodge, located at 5323 W Lake St in Chicago, Illinois has been closed by the City of Chicago due to numerous code violations.

Past Master Danny R. Williams Jr. of Port Royal Scott Lodge No. 591 of the Most Worshipful Prince Hall Grand Lodge of Georgia tells of his account in the spurious lodge he was a former member of, Jeff Long Grand Lodge in Georgia under the banner of reformed universal Masonic Brotherhood in October 2002.

"I still remember my IPR [initiating, passing, and raising] in my former bogus lodge, it was a rite of passage to get hit so hard with a paddle till the paddle breaks on your ass. I was 22 and I thought a masons degree work was like that. My raising my ass was all kinds of colors and had knots on it from "picking up the square" my girl asked me "what kind of mess you in I thought masons were grown men and not college kids pledging a frat" needless to say in the years to follow I became a master hazer myself from paddles to belts to hot peppers to dry ice. When I read the book morals and dogma in 2004 it changed my outlook and I no longer participated in hazing. The mentality is if I beat his ass he will love it more, that's bull I've seen guys hazed and not hazed and the attrition is the same."

Worshipful Brother Williams goes on to explain:

"My initiation was horrible as we were paddled while we were circumambulated around the room. It ended by us sealing our obligation and being hit while we bent over and kissed the bible. The second degree was worse. There was no middle chamber lecture, and the paddling was two times the amount. Plus, we were made to ingest wages that consisted of raw popcorn, prune juice, and olive oil. The third degree was basically an organized beating. We were paddled from start to finish and the sectors portion we were in our underwear and paddled. The obligation was given with stacks of chairs on our arms. We were also made to ingest habanero peppers and this hot sauce called "death."

"Study sessions in between degrees took place in a brother's basement. If you got an answer wrong you had to hold paint cans or do push-ups."

"In May of 2007, we did the second portion of a raising outside at a brother's private property in his back yard, which was about 15 acres. There were well over 50 brothers there for this raising and several bought homemade paddles. I was the Senior Deacon and there were five brothers being raised. They were being hit so hard that I could feel the breeze of the paddles as I passed by. After several trips around and finally when it was over, one of the newly raised said his back was hurting. He went to the restroom and urinated and that's when he saw the blood. Apparently his kidneys had been bruised. As for me I remember getting raised and literally having a double ass because of the swelling in my ass checks."

      A photo was leaked from a spurious Shriner ritual onto the internet which illustrates the terrible treatment of men desirous of becoming Shriners. It is too explicit to place in this book. It depicts a man being forced on to his hands and knees with a man sitting on his back holding a wooden paddle. In front of the man on his hands and knees is another man with his back towards the candidate, bent over, with his pants pulled down to expose his backside towards the face of the candidate.

The photo is alleged to be from Kabba Temple No. 1 in New Jersey, a spurious Shrine. The Potentate at the time of the release of this photo, Raymond R Edwards Sr., was named by several former members of the International Free and Accepted Modern Masons, who were members of International at the same time that he was, as the person that allowed such actions, lessons he learned as a former member of the International Free and Accepted Modern Masons.

This accusation was corroborated by numerous former members though Raymond declined to neither confirm nor deny that the action took place in his Shrine Temple. One must ask, what is the philosophical lesson to be gained by placing a person's head in the rear of another man, while paddling him on his backside? As a former spurious mason from 2004 until 2009 in Kankakee, Illinois at what was called St. Elmo Lodge no. 70A, which was renumbered as St. Elmo Lodge no. 916 subordinate to the Lee Cross Grand Council, another spurious organization, I was made a spurious Shriner and endured paddling as well, but not this grotesque treatment. I inquired about this incident with Mr. Raymond R. Edwards Sr. through social media, which was publicized. Here is a transcript of the interaction:

Conversation between Raymond Edwards and myself on May 27, 2014:

Charles M. Harper Sr., "Hello Raymond. My name is Charles Harper. I was given a photo by a confidential informant and while identifying the Shriners in the photo, your name has come to surface as the originator of the photo. Originally, my informant identified the photo as originating from an International Free and Accepted Modern Masons Shrine initiation. Robert Galburth, a member of this organization claims that it is not of the organization, but of a different group. I have been since contacted by others indicating that this photo attached is of your organization. Would you care to officially comment on the photo?"

Raymond R Edwards Sr., "Mr Harper I will respond to your request via telephone"

Charles M. Harper Sr., "The conversation cannot be confidential though as this interview is to clarify public comments. Are we in agreement?"

Raymond R Edwards Sr., "Then I respectfully decline. Things happen accidentally and we all must learn to judge as we want to be judged.. I will not participate in any negative propaganda by or towards any masonic body. Thanks. BE BLESSED."

Charles M. Harper Sr., "Then I have no choice but to acknowledge that you have declined to comment on the photo as having been identified as the source by a credible witness."

Raymond R Edwards Sr., "I have not confirmed or denied anything sir. You can do as you please which I'm quite sure us the case. What group or entity do you represent?"

Charles M. Harper Sr., "The Living Stones Magazine found at www.livingstonesmagazine.com. Your statements here is what I will be quoting. Nothing more."

Raymond R Edwards Sr., "Who is the owner of this entity?"

Charles M. Harper Sr., "Why? My source is credible so if you do not care to comment, that is what I will run in my article. You can contact the editor through the email provided in the link."

Raymond R Edwards Sr., "You can contact me and ask a question but I can't ask you one and not get a answer."

Charles M. Harper Sr., "You have not answered my question. You answer mine and I will answer yours."

Raymond R Edwards Sr., "OK who is you so called confidential informant?"

Charles M. Harper Sr., "No credible person making a report names a confidential informant. There are ethics to reporting. Not even the law can make a reporter divulge their sources. You have declined to comment so, there is not much more to discuss, unless you change your mind. All I am searching for is the truth. If you do not wish to give your truth, then what I have been able to corroborate will suffice."

Raymond R Edwards Sr., "OK thanks. .take care."

Charles M. Harper Sr., "I expose spurious masonic lodges and practices. What is depicted in the photo is assault and battery, and is against the law. My sources have indicated that you are the party responsible, and that you were a member of the International Free and Accepted Modern Masons. I am trying to identify if you did this before you left, or during your stint as the Grand Master of your new organization."

Raymond R Edwards Sr., "If you are sure that's me then do as you will. Spurious groups. Have you exposed PHA yet?"

Charles M. Harper Sr., "If you wish to make a comment, you can call the number provided that is connected to a recorder. The conversation would be recorded. You can clear the air if you would like."

Prince Hall Masonry is not spurious. They are regular and recognized by the United Grand Lodge of England as such."

Raymond R Edwards Sr., "Answer this.. Agreed that Prince Hall was issued a warrant for a Lodge.. But how was the Grand Lodge formed legitimately. That's spurious."

Charles M. Harper Sr., "No. An investigation was performed in 1992 as to the forming and perpetuation of the Prince Hall Grand Lodges in the United States by the United Grand Lodge of England. They have determined, and the report is available to the public, that though Prince Hall Grand Lodges were formed irregularly to today's accepted practices, the establishment of the Prince Hall Grand Lodges are consistent with the formation of Grand Lodges in the 18th century. The existing Grand Lodges accommodated the report and waived the Exclusive Territory Doctrine and accepted the report. Only 9 Grand Lodges have not waived this territorial doctrine."

Raymond R Edwards Sr., "I don't mind debating with educated masons. I just don't like have conversations with fellows that are just bent on destruction of other masonic groups especially

Africa American groups. So because you got a pass in 1992 you were not formed spuriously?"

Charles M. Harper Sr., "Spurious Masonry, specifically unregulated practiced Freemasonry that affects all of Freemasonry and more specifically amongst the African American Community, is illegal in most states and undermines the productivity of Prince Hall Masonry in the United States.. I will be giving a lecture on this subject at the New Jersey Masonic Symposium at the Valley of Southern New Jersey in September 2014."

Raymond R Edwards Sr., "But i do respect the fact that you answered honestly. That's more than your comrades have done in the past. Send me a invite. I might be able to attend."

Charles M. Harper Sr., "You will not be able to attend as your organization is not recognized as Masonic. Only mainstream and Prince Hall Masons are allowed in the tiled event. You can contact the event organizer for more information.

Raymond R Edwards Sr., "My question to you is that why do you feel that you will are going to attract men to pha when the members do no more than bash other groups and most are very uneducated in freemasonry."

Charles M. Harper Sr., "I am not interested in attracting men to Prince Hall or mainstream Freemasonry."

Raymond R Edwards Sr., "OK no problem with the invite. You mentioned it. I didn't. So your goal as a prince hall mason is to destroy the harmony and fellowship that black men have from the groups they belong to? That's not freemasonry! If you only knew how many PHA contact me to ask questions about freemasonry. You all need to spend more time writing lectures and teaching verses wasting to trying to destroy others."

Charles M. Harper Sr., "I am not a Prince Hall Mason. I am a member of the Grand Lodge of Illinois, and the United Grand Lodge of England. My goal is to eliminate illegally practiced Freemasonry that negatively affects the Fraternity of Freemasons that include Prince Hall Masons. It is the negativity caused by illegally practiced Freemasonry such as physical and mental hazing, and even in some cases deaths due to performing rituals not authorized by a regular and recognized Masonic Grand Lodge, that causes problems for both mainstream and Prince Hall Masonry. As you have not shown yourself to be a credible authority on either Freemasonry, or specifically the subject at hand, I will not be taking your word that Prince Hall Masons contact you for education. That statement will have to be corroborated by those Prince hall Masons you state have contacted you."

Raymond R Edwards Sr., "I wouldn't do that to them just because of the way you are handling this. You have no credibility either and have already shown that you have nothing in your heart and mind but fear of those that know more than you. Good luck in your quest for fame and notoriety."

Charles M. Harper Sr., "So be it. Good day."

This exchange is repeated ad nauseum daily on social media and in person by numerous Masons who are former spurious members, attempting to assist these men to legitimate Freemasonry. In every regular and well governed Lodge, a Master Mason is obligated and charged to remove every aspersion from the Masonic institution, and to correct the irregularities of less informed Brethren. A person is confronted about the irregular actions of their spurious organization, are presented information that disproves their assumptions, and they respond with character attacks rather than justify their assumptions with credible information. Thus, this exchange and the all too often repeating of it by Masons confronting spurious masons committing these atrocities from around the country, have caused them to grow incredibly frustrated at the empty and unproductive rhetoric. Defenses used by these groups to justify their conduct is that Prince Hall Shriners are performing these deeds as well.

From the Ancient Egyptian Arabic Order Nobles Mystic Shrine of North and South America and its Jurisdiction:

> The Ancient Egyptian Arabic Order Nobles Mystic Shrine, Inc. strictly prohibits hazing in any form, whether physical or mental, as a term or condition of membership in this organization. The A.E.A.O.N.M.S. Inc. does not consent to, condone, acquiesce, in or tolerate any act of hazing, harassment or humiliation of any candidate for admission into this organization.[xxxii]

This warning goes on to state that "Hazing is illegal and a crime in most jurisdictions." Accordingly, just as Shriners International has a strict no-hazing policy, the Prince Hall Shriners have taken the same stance to protect the integrity of Shrinedom. The form also states the definition of hazing to leave no ambiguity as to what it is, and what one is not allowed to do stating hazing is:

> Any action taken or situation created, intentionally, to produce mental or physical discomfort, embarrassment, harassment or ridicule. Such activities may include but are not limited to the following: use of alcohol; paddling in any form; creation of excessive fatigue; physical and psychological shocks, quests, or any other such activities carried on; wearing of public apparel which is conspicuous and not normally in good taste; and any other activities which are not consistent with A.E.A.O.N.M.S., Inc. policy or ritual.

While there used to be some forms of hazing mentioned in relation to all Shriners which were better described as pranks that were not humiliating and all in good fun, no person was injured and hazing in any manner or form has been long since forbidden. I am a member of Medinah Shriners in Addison, Illinois, and my creation was delightful and philosophically explained. Most of the ritual except for the passwords, signs, and grips, are actually often done in public before the families and friends of the candidates. Prince Hall Shriners do not perform public rituals as Shriners International allows. These have been examples of the physical and ideologies held by spurious leaders of fraudulent organizations who have falsely justified their actions using the Prince Hall Shriners as scapegoats, which we have now disproven. Let us explore the financial aspect of spurious Freemasonry.

Organizations such as the International Free and Accepted Modern Masons commit fraud in deceiving its members into believing they share the same history as Shriners International, the masonic organization that funds the Shriner Children Hospitals. From the International Free and Accepted Modern Masons Website:

> The Shrine is an international fraternity of approximately 775,000 members who belong to Shrine Temples throughout the United States, Canada and Mexico. Founded in New York City in 1872, the organization is composed solely of 32nd

degree Scottish Rite Masons or Knights Templar York Rite Masons. Each and every year, International Shriners donate time, money, and resources to assist children in hospitals, provide medical care support for women, men, and children, as well as provide school supplies and toys to youth and young adults.[xxxiii]

It goes on to state:

> The Turner S. Hartfield Supreme Imperial Council works very hard to ensure that our members understand the basics of the Ancient Arabic Order of the Nobles of the Mystic Shrine, also commonly known as Shriners and abbreviated A.A.O.N.M.S. Established in 1870, is an appendant body to Freemasonry, based in the United States. We work with our Masonic brothers from the foundation house all the way up to the Holy Empire to ensure that Masonry and Shrinedom has the best representation when it comes to faith, hope and charity.
>
> The Turner S. Hartfield Supreme Imperial Council is overseen by Illustrious Michael C. Webster, 33°. His role is to work with Potentates in educating,

sharing, nurturing, and developing relationships throughout the entire country and areas the organization has a presence that assists in building the image of the department and organization overall.

For more information about this Department, you can contact Illustrious Michael C. Webster, 33° - Supreme Imperial Potentate via phone at 414-232-2110 or email him at: imperial_council@internationalmasons.org.

To provide a separation between spurious Freemasonry misrepresented or misinterpreted by mainstream Masons and the public, on January 1974, Volume 1 Number 1 of the Phylaxis magazine, created by Joseph A. Walked Jr., would be published. In it, it stated that "too often information concerning Prince Hall Masonry is written by those who have little knowledge of Masonry in general and Prince Hall Masonry in particular." It goes on to state that the "official position of the Phylaxis Society" is that "research into all phases of Prince Hall Masonry is truly needed, and that the true history of Prince Hall Masonry must be written by Prince Hall Masons themselves."[xxxiv] Joseph A. Walkes Jr. was the author of

Black Square and Compass, 200 years of Prince Hall Freemasonry, as well as *Prince Hall's Mission*.

The exposing of bogus masonic practices has rested squarely on the shoulders of Joseph Walkes and other members of the Prince Hall Grand Lodges, the issue long perceived as a "Black problem" due to cultural isolation and an inability to impress the seriousness of this issue upon all regular grand lodges in the United States because of a lack of intercultural communication and understanding existing in the Fraternity. Masons such as Ralph McNeal Jr., Ezekiel Bey, and others of the Phylaxis Society have carried on the campaign against spurious Masonry for years with others now carrying the torch such as Antoine Lilly, Council of Representatives President of the Commission on Bogus Masonic Practices and John Hairston of the Prince Hall Grand Lodge of Washington. To also be included are Brother Ed King of Maine, giving information from his website www.masoincinfo.com. With all their efforts and those in their assistance, it will not be enough to combat this negative epidemic undermining the moral progression of our Fraternity if the potential victims of these organizations are not informed in the most efficient manner possible- a display of unity against spurious masonry amongst all regular Grand Lodges in the United States.

My Brethren, now is the time to remove our heads from the sands and cease to act as if this growing problem of spurious masonry, who does not just prey on unknowing non-masons who want to become masons but regularly made masons alike who seem dissatisfied with the lack of education or ethnic composition of our lodges, does not need our attention. Please educate every Grand Lodge and warn your members of these spurious masonic grand lodges and obtain legal proof of membership before speaking or visiting anyone claiming to be a mason. If your Grand Lodge has not trademarked the Square and Compass, do it!

It was suggested by the Masonic Service Association in 1992 that all Grand Lodges now trademark the square and compass. There are more Grand Lodges overseas that have complied with this warning than Grand Lodges within the United States. New York, Connecticut, and several other states have actual codes of law that are simply not enforced or known about. Not all Grand Lodges can approach this problem through state government, such as Illinois, but individual members can. Court rulings substantiate that there is legal protection at least by the state courts. Here are some examples listed in the Short Talk Bulletin of December 1935 from the Masonic Service Association of North America

> The conviction in the Federal Court at Salt Lake City, Utah, on May 15, 1922, of Matthew A. McBlain Thomson, Thomas Perrot and Dominic Bergera, of using the mails to defraud, was the culmination of efforts of the United States Government, begun in 1915, to have a reckoning with the perpetrators of one of the most ingenious mail frauds, and the most daring and spectacular Masonic imposture in American history.
>
> In 1929 there was filed in the office of the Secretary of State of New Jersey a Certificate of Incorporation of "The Grand Lodge of Ancient Free and Accepted Masons of New Jersey," under which certificate the incorporators claimed the right to:
>
> "Practice and preserve Ancient Craft Masonry according to the Ancient Charges, Constitutions and Land Marks of Free Masonry; to create, organize and supervise subordinate Lodges of Ancient Free and Accepted Masons, granting to them dispensations and charters, empowering them to

confer the degrees of Entered Apprentice, Fellowcraft and Master Mason; and to do all things necessary to carry into effect the objects and purposes of this incorporation."

The regular Grand Lodge instituted suit in the Court of Chancery against this spurious Grand Lodge with the result that in 1932 there was entered a decree restraining and enjoining this "Grand Lodge of ancient Free and accepted Masons of New Jersey," its officers, agents, members and employees,

1. From using the name or designation "The Grand Lodge of Ancient Free and Accepted Masons of New Jersey."

2. From using any name or designation containing the words "Free and Accepted Masons," or word "Mason," or "Masons," in conjunction with either or both of the words "Free and Accepted."

3. From practicing, or pretending to practice Ancient Craft Masonry, according to the ancient Charges, Constitutions and Land Marks of Free Masonry; from creating, organizing or supervising subordinate Lodges of Free and Accepted Masons

in the State of New Jersey, or pretending to do so; from conferring or pretending to confer the three degrees of Free Masonry known as Entered Apprentice, Fellowcraft and Master Mason, or any of them.

South Dakota once had an Italian spurious body, but it has disbanded. Texas has to contend with the clandestine Mexican bodies. Utah has had some experiences, but her most famous contribution to the history of clandestine Masonry was the trial of the notorious McBain and Thompson. That Masonic fraud was there exposed and the perpetrators sent to jail. M.W. Sam H. Goodwin, Grand Secretary, writes of this: "Grand Lodge has not entered the arena against clandestinism, but a great battle against clandestinism was brought to a successful conclusion in the Federal Court in Salt Lake City, and the chief promoters of the Thompson Masonic Fraud (three in number) heard a jury declare them guilty, on ten counts, of using the U.S. Mails to defraud.

In a majority of States, legislation has been passed making it an offense and against the law to use the

emblems of a fraternal organization without a right, or to adopt and use the name of a pre-existent fraternal, charitable, benevolent, humane or other non-profit making organization. Some of these laws are very elaborate, others are less specific, but in States where such legislation has been invoked by regular Masonry against usurpation by clandestine bodies, the courts have upheld, or are now in the process of upholding the regular and recognized Grand Lodges of the nation against those who would profit at their expense.[xxxv] There have been state rulings against spurious masonry, filed by Grand Lodges, since before the 1950's by Prince Hall Grand Lodges.
http://www.thephylaxis.org/bogus/masonicourtcases.php

Silence or ignoring the existence of these organizations will not help this ever growing problem. As I state in my lectures, the problems that we do not confront within our precious fraternity acts as termites within a tree. They will continue to erode the inside of that tree and when least expected, a strong wind will blow, and the tree will collapse. Let us strengthen our tree Brethren with education and protection so that future generations will be fed by the fruits it can produce. In the next chapter, we will explore why this epidemic of spurious Freemasonry has endured, seemingly unimpeded in America.

Chapter 3
Prejudice and Discrimination Practiced in Freemasonry

The word prejudice is a harsh sounding word, especially in the world of Freemasonry. Discrimination is just as harsh. The general understanding of Freemasonry given to the public is that we are a fraternity that is welcoming to men of all faiths, ethnicities, and various backgrounds. For the most part, here in the 21st century, that is a private and public truth. It is not always a reality practiced in private amongst some of the more isolated lodges where various ethnicities do not comprise the membership and prevents circumstances where ideologies can be challenged. Before examining discriminatory practices that aid the growth of spurious Freemasonry in the United States, I am going to call attention to prejudicial societal mindsets.

The social aspect I am going to bring forth first in this chapter is that of a discriminatory mindset that seeks to restrict the freedom to practice the speculation of conceived ideas formulated by masonic study in the aspects of masonic ritual. I will then show how this failure to allow the concept of the interpretation of speculative Freemasonry to be practiced potentially voids the transformative process from occurring, and further perpetuates acts either consciously or subconsciously of discrimination.

What does the word prejudice mean? From the Merriam-Webster dictionary, it is explained as a "feeling of like or dislike for someone or something especially when it is not reasonable or logical." In this respect, no matter how one may wish to present himself in being free of prejudicial thoughts, we are all guilty of this in one respect or another. Though we may feel as Masons we have mastered logic and the subduing of our passions, the mastering of feelings is a difficult task even on our best day. "I do not like that color "or "I feel like he should not speak to his child in that manner," are examples of exercising a decision made from a general feeling, rather than one placed against the equation of logic. It is difficult to debate with another person their feelings about something that is inconsequential because their feelings are a part of their core beliefs. As much as one may not like or want to believe it, these are examples of exhibiting prejudice.

A result of prejudiced feelings or thoughts played into motion in some variation is the act of discrimination. The Gale Group describes discrimination as being a differential or unequal treatment of a particular group. Groups are usually distinguished or divided along religious, ethnic, political or among racial lines. Discrimination is not limited to major categories as it extends to subgroups such as age, gender, and sexual persuasion, all which can be potentially discriminated against. Discrimination can be viewed as a continuum or a scale. At one end lies less severe forms of discrimination (verbal assault, denial of resources), and at the other end, more severe forms of discrimination are located (physical aggression, genocide). All other forms of discrimination lie at some point on this continuum."[xxxvi]

As we are all charged as Master Masons to correct the irregularities of our less informed Brethren, how often do we consider that what we feel is in fact irregular, is just that? Do we stop to question if it is a feeling of prejudice, or a resolve based upon logic? It is easy to suggest that a Brother not visit a clandestine lodge, or that he should exercise the charity of giving time to a laudable cause, for those are readily acceptable confrontations. But, how do we confront a Brother who displays a prejudice based on his belief when it can be proven by logic that their thought or action is in fact irregular? Men who are culturally isolated can make decisions based upon their perception rather than factual understanding that results in an act of discrimination for which he may not even be aware. The answer is logic explained in a manner that is culturally relevant to an individual's understanding.

Culturally relevant logic used in confrontation must be based on proportional knowledge, not associative or direct based knowledge. The latter two can be given with bias and may not allow a Brother to come to an understanding he can accept of his own free will and accord that will cause progressive change in his convictions. Epistemology, the branch of philosophy concerned with the nature and scope of knowledge, is essential as the foundation in determining what is actual and can be academically substantiated, what is derived from hearsay, or what is learned by trial and error for a mason to establish his facts before engaging in speculation. As much as one may feel uncomfortable with the idea of confronting another Brother, we are actually obligated too. A whisper? Yes, even the whisper is a confrontation. The catechism? Yes, it is a confrontation as one is asked a question to determine if the respondent is equipped with a properly memorized understanding. It is a responsibility that is not desirable to execute, but without, the Craft would veer so far from its original intent that it would become what it was not intended to be.

As the situation of spurious Freemasonry and exclusion to membership of a lodge predicated on one's ethnicities or sexuality have started to publically present themselves in fashions unprecedented due to the internet. We are now confronted with developing schisms of masonic dispositions towards what specifically are the components that comprise traditional speculative freemasonry, and what separates its practices from those of any other social order. Sound familiar? It should.

In 1751 Lawrence Dermott, elected Grand Secretary of Grand Lodge of the Ancients in England, felt the same way. The first Grand Lodge organized in 1717, known in history as the Moderns, became selective in its membership and would only allow Aristocrats as members, and excluded Irish and Scots tradesmen from membership. It moved away from the Ancient tradition of all men being equal and judged by their internal qualities and not the external. It was a more modern way of thinking, far from the tenants of the ancient ideas. The Fraternity had become a social fraternity with festive boards fully stocked with food and libations where ritual and philosophical discussions were replaced with laughter and politicking for a time. As occurrences in history repeat themselves, just as the tide of the ocean rises and falls twice each day, we are once again upon a surge of disagreement involving what are ancient practices of the Craft and what has been a social mindset infesting the craft causing discriminative practices that has existed for many years. They are being weighed and measured in the eyes of the public and should be giving Freemasons a moment of pause and reflection of our behavior.

Providing such evidence as some practicing discriminatory practices in the eyes of the public is not difficult. "White-controlled Grand Lodges in 12 Southern states do not even officially recognize black Masons as their brothers — the Masonic term is "mutual recognition" — and in some cases, black lodges have taken similar stands. Masons have quietly debated race relations for years, and the issue is increasingly coming into public view." This was a report by NBC Nightly News on October 24, 2006. Since 2006, both Texas and Kentucky Grand Lodges have established mutual recognition, but without visitation. As of the summer of 2014, the two

Grand Lodges in Texas have made some advancements to establish visitation as well. This would be wise and masonic for all the members of both jurisdictions who desire to take advantage of inter-visitation.

In 2009, as mentioned in my previous book Freemasonry in Black and White, which is Volume I in this series of the exploration of moral progression of the masonic institution, Victor Marshall of Gate City Lodge No. 2 in Atlanta, Georgia under the jurisdiction of the Grand Lodge of Georgia became well known as the first African-American made a Master Mason in a regularly constituted Lodge subordinate to that grand lodge. This was public news as well in the July 2, 2009, an article by the New York Times entitled *"Black Member Tests Message of Masons in Georgia Lodges,"* written by Shaila Dewan and Robbie Brown.

> The members of the Gate City Lodge No. 2 would like it known that Freemasonry, a centuries-old fraternal organization founded on the principles of the Enlightenment, is not racist. But some of their fellow Masons here in Georgia are spoiling the message.

> In June, the Worshipful Master, or leader, of the Gate City Lodge was served with complaints from two other lodges, whose Worshipful Masters were upset that Gate City had admitted a "nonwhite man" to its ranks.
>
> Although the rules of Freemasonry do not say that members must be white, and there are numerous Hispanics, Asians and other ethnicities represented in lodges across the state, the Grand Master of Georgia decreed that the complaints would be heard in a Masonic trial that could have resulted in expulsion of a lodge or members of it. In response, Gate City (the name is an old nickname for Atlanta) filed a lawsuit in state court seeking an injunction to prevent its charter from being revoked.[xxxvii]

The article goes on to state:

> Despite its principles of tolerance, Freemasonry in the United States has historically been divided between so-called mainstream Masons and traditionally black Prince Hall Masons.

This is in a nationally respected newspaper. Attempts at establishing mutual recognition were efforted by the Prince

Hall Grand Lodge of Georgia, which is also stated in the article:

> Five or six years ago, [the year 2000] the Prince Hall Masons in Georgia approached the mainstream Masons about recognition, said Ramsey Davis Jr., Grand Master of the Prince Hall Grand Lodge in Riverdale, Ga. But the group was not interested, Mr. Davis said.

This is an act of discrimination inspired by prejudice. It is an example of generationally taught prejudice held within the culture of that demographic which negatively affects a masonic lodge that exists to make all men equal, where that displayed ideology should never be tolerated in any capacity. If it should not be tolerated and it is against masonic precepts, why does it exist? The answer is cultural isolation. The Masonic Lodge is a subculture existing within the culture in which it is physically established. It is a microcosm of society. A subculture within a greater culture. Lodges exist within communities. If the community is diverse and the lodge membership isn't, it could be that the lodge is either intentionally or unintentionally, allowing themselves to be culturally isolated, a subculture within a culture.

This isolated culture, or lodge that has existed in an environment that was naturally isolated due to the effects of slavery and then segregation after 1865, has never had to either worry about African-Americans petitioning their lodge or having a conversation within its doors that had anything to do with African-Americans ever potentially desiring to become members. As can be often hear in the South, as well in isolated areas around the nation, "We have our lodges and they have their lodges. We stay with our kind, they stay with their kind." This mentality contradicts the precepts of the masonic institution 100%! There is "no kind" with regards to Masons. Masonic ritual specifies that it is the internal and not the external part of man that qualifies him for membership.

In the same referenced article, a mention is made of "a West Virginia Masonic leader was expelled for proposing to loosen the rules that kept the state's mainstream chapters all white." The two men involved in this disgraceful incident was Brother Raymond Sean Walters and Frank Haas, the latter to that date of this writing is still an expelled Past Grand Master of the Grand Lodge of West Virginia who was expelled without a Masonic trial.

From the Edict of M.W. Charlie Law Montgomery

Grand Master of Masons:

EDICT

Expelling Frank J. Haas of Wellsburg Lodge No. 2

To: The Worshipful Masters, Wardens and Brethren of the subordinate lodges of the Most Worshipful Grand Lodge A. F. & A. M. of the State of West Virginia

Brethren:

There is a coalition of brethren and members of concordant bodies within the Grand Jurisdiction of West Virginia that has come to be known as the Masonic Crusade. The activities of this coalition consist mainly of campaigning, recruiting, advertisement of false information and unauthorized circulation. Furthermore, these activities have disrupted the peace and harmony of the craft and to demonstrate intent to control this Grand Lodge and do violate and circumvent our laws, rules, regulations and the obligations to which all West Virginia Masons are bound.

Whereas, our Masonic Law speaks to these offenses in Articles II and XI of our Code of Trials (CT.II, Sec. 1., CT.II.1.17., CT.II.1.20., CT.II.1.24.and CT.XI., Sec. 2.), Regulations 24.F.15., 31 (31.9), 39 (A.10.) and our Landmark number five: Know ye that by virtue of the authority vested in me in Article III of the Constitution of the Most Worshipful Grand Lodge of A. F. & A. M. of the State of West Virginia, Inc., our Landmark number four and elsewhere as provided under our laws, I Charlie Law Montgomery, hereby order and reaffirm that participation in the affairs of the Masonic Crusade, including participation in its illegal website activities, or any related endeavor, constitutes un-Masonic conduct and will be treated as such.

Whereas, Frank J. Haas has participated in the affairs of the Masonic Crusade, and has incited, endorsed, aided, abetted and perpetuated the same, and whereas Frank J. Haas did on December 2, 2006, October 26, 2007 and on other occasions, speak to delegations of concordant bodies where the profane were also present, and did on such occasions propose and advocate support for amendments and repeal of our laws, such activity being strictly prohibited under CT.II.1.20. of our Code of Trials, and whereas

Frank J. Haas did on August 30, 2007 circulate email promoting and encouraging the affairs of the Masonic Crusade, and whereas Frank J. Haas did during the week of October 1 through 6, 2007 promote, contact and encourage other brethren to participate and subscribe to the illegal website of the Masonic Crusade, and whereas Frank J. Haas, during the One Hundred and Forty Third Annual Communication of the Grand Lodge of West Virginia, and on numerous occasions during the year preceding such Annual Communication, did endeavor to gain voting support for amendments and repeal of our laws as well as voting support to subvert the principles of the order and the actions of the Grand Lodge and Grand Master, and whereas Frank J. Haas, on November 5, 2007 and on other occasions, has been publicly insubordinate and disrespectful toward the Grand Lodge, its Grand Master and other Grand Lodge Officers, and has demonstrated conduct unbecoming a Mason in this Grand Jurisdiction.[xxxviii]

What is the Masonic Crusade? From the Masonic Crusade website:

As an Internet Society the Masonic Crusade believes in the following:

1. Truth, Justice, and Tolerance are indispensable qualities of Leadership and Membership

2. Transparent, and open Government of Our Fraternity with Freedom of opinion and Equal participation by all

3. Education and Participation are essential for Harmonious and Equitable Brotherhood

4. Reformation of the Laws, and General Regulations to bring West Virginia Masonry into accord with modern Masonic Jurisprudence.

5. Insuring Preservation of the Ancient Landmarks, Customs and Usages of the Fraternity

6. Support of lawful legislative efforts to bring about positive change and growth in Our Fraternity.[xxxix]

To streamline the expulsion of Frank Haas, the formation of this website and its purpose, and to show how the unmasonic prejudicial attitudes have spilled into the public by a Grand Lodge's own actions giving a horrid and inaccurate representation of Freemasonry, here is a narrow summery of actual events.

Raymond Walters, a Master Mason in good standing at the time in both the Grand Lodge of Texas and the Grand Lodge of North Carolina by way of plural memberships, attempted to visit a Lodge in West Virginia. The Lodge refused him entrance even into the building shouting vulgar racial comments as the reason he was not wanted inside the building. This shouting of racial slurs to Raymond occurred in the view of the public as the lodge resides next to a McDonald's restaurant and availed the customers of it to witness the exchange. The result of this exchange was a resolution passed at the 2006 Grand Lodge of West Virginia Grand Communication in which Frank Haas, the Grand Master at the time, put forth many resolutions hopefully to be enacted which would morally progress the practices of West Virginian Freemasonry. Some of the proposals were:

1. Plural membership: Allowing our members to join more than one lodge, in any grand jurisdiction with which we are in fraternal communication, and allowing our lodges to accept as members brothers, who will retain their membership in another regular lodge, in any grand jurisdiction with which we are in fraternal communication, will add strength to the lodges by brothers who thereby voluntarily increase their Masonic dues and commitment.

2. Wavier of Territorial Jurisdiction by a majority vote: Our laws protecting territorial jurisdiction were developed to prevent disputes between lodges over initiation fees, which at one time amounted to two-week's gross wages on the average. When measured by the workweek, our fees now are much lower. In former times, transportation and

communication were far more difficult. Then, making an assessment of a man's character was most likely to be accurate only at his place of residence, which was also his place of work and which was also his place of worship. Our society has changed. There are many good reasons for a man to seek membership in a lodge that is not the closest to his residence.

3. Disabled petitioners and candidates: no longer valid. The prohibition was used to prevent a problem that no longer exists. Now, the main effect of the enforcement of the prohibition is to keep good men out of Freemasonry, contrary to its original laudable purpose. Proper inquiry is to be made of a petitioner's means of support. Physical disabilities should not be a categorical bar to membership.

4. Frank Haas notes that West Virginia is the only Grand Lodge not a member of the MSA. A motion will be made for the Most Worshipful Grand Lodge of Ancient, Free and Accepted Masons of the State of West Virginia to join as a contributing member

of the Masonic Service Association of North America.

In support of the moral progressive mindset of the Grand Lodge under Frank Haas, the following Rulings were referred to the Committee on Masonic Jurisprudence, and the following Rulings and were effective immediately.

The second ruling stated that "Qualified visiting brethren may not be excluded from attendance if race is a factor." It goes on to support this ruling with notes from Masonic Ritual teachings stating "We learn in the Entered Apprentice's Degree that "Freemasonry unites men of every country, sect, and opinion." It would be contrary to the most basic principle of freemasonry to exclude from attending a lodge in West Virginia a Mason who has been initiated, passed, and raised in a Grand Lodge with which we are in fraternal communication. In fact, to maintain recognition by such other Grand Lodge, our Grand Lodge has made the commitment to admit a member of the other Grand Jurisdiction provided he could prove such membership and returns the Tiler's Oath. Masters of Lodges in the Grand Jurisdiction of West Virginia are, therefore, reminded that it would be unmasonic to exclude from attendance any member of a lodge from another grand jurisdiction with which we are in fraternal communication on the grounds of his nationality, race, or religion.[xl]

This was the ruling in direct response to the exclusion of Brother Raymond Walters from visiting the West Virginian Lodge. Two weeks later, all measures passed in the Grand Session were set aside by the newly elected Grand Master. This is an example of prejudicial mindsets clearly demonstrated by discrimination, resulting in a regression of morality taught or practiced by the Grand Lodge of West Virginia. God help the West Virginian Masons who feel differently and to stay beneath the radar of Grand Lodge, or other Masons who support the grand lodge's rulings, as they are the oppressed subculture within this culture of Freemasonry. One has to be disgusted at how this behavior could ever come to be acceptable in any Masonic Lodge or Grand Lodge. The results are the Grand Lodges own doing.

On June 12, 2012, the Grand Master of the Masonic Grand Lodge of New South Wales and Australian Capital Territory issued an edict concerning esoteric studies in the Masonic Fraternity. The edict stating:

GRAND MASTER'S EDICT

ANNOUNCED AT THE GRAND COMMUNICATION – 13th JUNE, 2012

On 12 May 2010 the Board of Management passed a resolution stating the principles governing esoteric research. These principles are central to the practice of Regular Freemasonry. In order that there be no doubt that they bind every brother and Lodge in this jurisdiction I have decided to make them the subject of a Grand Master's edict. At my request the Board of Management has rescinded its resolution so that it may be substituted with the following edict which takes effect immediately.

1. Authorized, official Masonic Education and Instruction is only 'Regular' when applied to Free and Accepted or Speculative Masonry (Regular Freemasonry).

2. Because of the widely divergent interpretations which can be placed upon it, I am concerned about the unqualified use of the word "esoteric", or any of its derivatives or extensions, within Regular Freemasonry. Such use needs to be avoided as it has been and can be misconstrued to the detriment of the Craft.

3. I encourage all Masons to make daily progress in the acquisition of Masonic knowledge. Speculation and discussion within the Landmarks of the Order are to be commended.

4. Within Regular Freemasonry, interpretive discussion and exposition concern only the

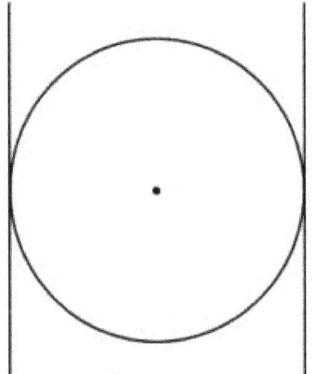

progressive acquisition of Masonic knowledge towards an understanding of the secrets and mysteries of the Craft, promoting the brotherhood of man under the fatherhood of God. To avoid any misapprehension, such regular discussion and exposition shall be described as "speculative" and the term "esoteric" shall not be applied.

This is where the feelings affect logical decisions of the Grand Master and it becomes a problem. To suggest that the word "esoteric" not be used and "speculate" should in masonic discussion is a fallacy and not a logical conclusion. When one speculates, they are guessing at the intent of a meaning. They are searching for that which is not readily seen. They are in fact, searching for the esoteric meaning in which to understand and apply masonic ritual and symbolism. How they relate to these teachings derives from the understanding of where the teachings originate, thus making them more applicable in the proper context to the individual Mason.

If I am to circumscribe myself within due bounds of all mankind, especially a Brother Mason, I must first apply that definition to the symbol implying the meaning. Then I must ascertain what the due bounds are in relation to my impression of the Divine Moral Law, or my Volume of Sacred Law, and establish the distance of my due bounds. This is speculation to define an esoteric meaning to apply the tenets of Masonic education. The words speculate and esoteric are not interchangeable to lesson confusion, they are cause and effect for one needs to DO the first to FIND the second, and take Action on the results.

5. Regular Freemasonry does not permit within it any form of esotericism which encompasses or tends towards – occultism, sorcery, alchemy, astrology, profane mysticism, transcendentalism, supernaturalism, druidism, rosicrucianism, Satanism or any concept or movement related to any of these. The presentation, endorsement and/or promotion of such subjects in any Lodge holding under the UGL of NSW and ACT whether the Lodge be open, adjourned, at refreshment or closed or at any connected or associated Lodge function should be deemed irregular and is strictly forbidden.

We see here again when the Grand Master states that "Regular Freemasonry" does not permit any form of esotericism. His examples reduce the merit of his opinion. The ancient landmarks that all regular Masonic jurisdictions adhere to defines what Freemasonry is in practice. What Freemasonry is philosophically is where from which ritual is derived. When William Preston wrote the first authorized ritual in 1776, he referenced both Masonry Dissected for the catechism it contained as to give guidance of how all lodges were initiating men into the speculative Craft, but he also relied heavily on the symbolism and philosophy of the Egyptians, Rosicrucians, Alchemist, Greeks, Sufi's, and Kabbalistic philosophy, and this is proven by simply showing our symbols and the meaning applied to them.

Of the Greeks, we received all the philosophy found within the liberal arts and sciences, predicated on the basis the Egyptian mystery schools and our friend Pythagoras. Of Alchemy, the practice of the transformation of a rude metal from one state to that of the purest metal which is gold, is that not the practice of taking an operative method and thus applying the symbolic meaning to it? We transform the individual's conscious and subconscious thoughts from one state of rudeness, to that of the highest quality. The refusal to allow one to see this analogy in relation to their own convictions is to eliminate a perfect example of the ability for a man to SEE how he can apply masonic meaning to his life. We, as Free and Accepted Masons, take the operative functions and make use of them for a more noble and glorious purpose.

    6. Any breach of this Edict constitutes serious unmasonic conduct and shall be treated accordingly.

7. The Grand Master from time to time may grant dispensations to permit the presentation of papers on esotericism which would otherwise constitute a breach of this edict. A dispensation may be granted on such terms and conditions as the Grand Master may impose. An application for a dispensation must be made to the Grand Master in writing through the Grand Secretary. Normally it will only be granted if the proposed paper is a genuine and proper piece of masonic research.[xli]

Unfortunately, it appears this edict has been applauded by some Grand Masters in the United States as well. In 2013, I received though an anonymous source that a charge had been levied against the Deputy Grand Master of the Grand Lodge of Colorado Dan Gannon, as he was threatening to remove esoteric practices from the Grand Lodge of Colorado. In this anonymous message, it was stated that the Traditional Observance Lodges, and those of a similar practicing nature meaning education and Brotherly Love with a more than 100% attendance in every lodge of its kind supported by ancient practices such as the Chamber of Reflection, may have their Charters removed. I was directed to a blog where it was stated:

"Dan Gannon's outspokenness of Masonic education is well documented. From official visits to my Lodge where he chided education as "a waste of time" to this year's grand Lodge session when he stated "Masonry is not esoteric" Dan Gannon not only disapproves of deeper reflection into our most sacred tenets and symbols but endeavored to shut down the activities of the Education Committee, silence the Masonic Speakers Bureau, and discontinue any enrichment he considers "esoteric crap." Dan Gannon publically stated that as Grand Master he would pull the charters of lodges that have any sort of progressive practices or educational events that he does not support. These practices included any Lodge that emphasized research, education, or best-practices."[xlii]

The Grand Lodge of Colorado Masons obviously did not support the ideas presented by Brother Dan Gannon as he lost the election to a Mason who was not even on the ballot. A Grand Officer who had previously withdrawn from the office of Senior Grand Warden, Michael McMillian was nominated. After balloting four times in two days, Brother McMillian, a staunch supporter of masonic education, was elected Grand Master of Masons in Colorado for the 2014 year.

This trend is nothing new. As I have stated before, it has happened in the past. The ramifications caused an "us versus them," amongst Freemasons that lasted for 62 years between 1751, and the uniting of the two prominent English Grand Lodges in London, England in 1813. The prevalent attitude, perpetuated by a lack of education as to the history of ancient knowledge that forms the basis of masonic ritual, or the denial of it, is once again causing a rift of epic proportions. Is epic too grand of a word to use? Maybe. But, when one considers the tangible effects of denying esoteric study as an essential part of Masonic education, the ramifications can be seen to be epic if one considers the negative effects it can have on the fraternity to thrive on the shoulders of this new generation of Masons.

Let me be clear in the labeling of this act. It is an action that clearly is a prejudicial and discriminatory act against those who seek more education from the Masonic institution that is a departure from the social club it had become. This resulted from the influx of masons joining, reaching its peak in 1959 and using the fraternity more for comradery than enlightenment. These practices were passed down to the next generation. Men, a generation separated from the previous by a gap of men joining, seek what Albert Pike sought- enlightenment. This episode in Colorado should serve to inform all Officers whether in Lodge or Grand Lodge, members compose the organization, not the officers elected to represent them. Also, progressive moral change is inevitable and one can fight change and become the outcast, or see the beauty and assist in it coming to fruition.

There is no logic to substantiate the creation of a law forbidding esoteric study, only the feeling of fear. This fear is that of change. Though change can be a worry, it is a fact that change is inevitable. The fact is even if a Grand Master were to forbid esoteric study, he technically cannot prevent its practice unless he removes ritual from being conducted in Lodge. For every time the masonic lecture is given in any of the three degrees of Craft Freemasonry, the lecturer is revealing to the candidate the hidden meanings of our symbols, the initial "secrets" of Freemasonry. Remember, the definition of esoteric is that which is only taught to or can be understood by members of a special group. Is not the members of the Craft members of a small or special group, and our ritual and symbols only to be understood by us? The answer is definitively- Yes.

I now draw your attention to the matter of the ritualistic reference of the Volume of Sacred Law described in many rituals as the Holy Bible. Far too often the fraternity appears to be presented by masons publically in social media, and privately in conversation, to be a Christian/Judaic organization. Having traveled a bit masonically and engaging in conversations in an explorative manner in the areas of religion and its effect on the lodge, in progressive circles the attitude of the acceptance of men of all faiths is quite the norm.

Having said that, there are an overabundance of conservative mindsets that proudly establish their criteria for a man to be welcomed to petition their Lodge. One of my most recent conversations in early 2014, a Mason explained his convictions to me proudly at a public event. He stated, "For a man to be accepted into my lodge, he first must be Christian, secondly an American, and third, a conservative." Is it his fault that he has the convictions? Some would say yes as he should have learned that two out of the three requirements have nothing to do with Freemasonry in the United States. And more specifically, under the Grand Lodge code to which this member is obliged, the requirements of residence is only that he be a member of his state for six months or more, and that he believe in a Supreme Being. However, his mindset is a result of an existence within an isolated culture, never engaged or challenged with ideologies in its privacy that have differed in supportive numbers, opposite in nature to this member's own.

As in all things to be understood properly in context, we must go back in history to find the source, and work our way forward. When did the word "Holy" first precede the word "Bible," and become part of Masonic ritual? Those without study would have you believe that the words Holy Bible were always a part of ritual, if you are to believe that Christianity is the foundation of Freemasonry. The fact is that the words Holy Bible, used together, was not added to masonic ritual in any capacity until Thomas Webb added it in his rendition of William Preston's written ritual of 1776.

> "In 1797 he attracted attention through a book titled "Freemason's Monitor or Illustrations of Masonry". In 1813 he became Grand Master of the Grand Lodge of Rhode Island. He is the real founder of

the so-called American Ritus which he developed in that form like it is cultivated in America even today."[xliii]

William Preston was authorized by the Grand Lodge of England to write a formal standardized ritual for all subordinate lodges under the constitution of the Grand Lodge of England to use. Before any written work, Lodges even prior to 1723 were using different manners to initiate men into the Craft. At one point, the Grand Master disallowed anyone to make a man a Master Mason, though allowing them to initiate men, as a means to standardize how a Man was made a Master Mason. Men were initiated in Lodge, but until 1734, they had to be raised at the Grand Lodge. The existence of the word Bible was in Preston's Ritual, which can be read in its entirety in his work Illustrations of Freemasonry.

The etymology of the word Bible has its origins from the Egyptians. It was initially the word "Byblos" meaning Egyptian papyrus. As we know that the Greek philosopher Pythagoras studied well the mystery schools of Egypt, we can see how the Greeks came to use this word and transitioned it use into their language calling the Bible- "biblion," meaning "paper or scroll." William Preston, using the expose Masonry Dissected by Samuel Pritchard, written in 1733, as his guide for his authorized ritual, which contained the word "Bible" in its catechism, added the word Bible representing a Holy Book of Moral Law as an indispensable furniture of the Lodge. It is reasonable to presume Preston knew the root meaning of the word as he was an avid student of Greek philosophy and Egyptian symbolism, evident by his numerous references in both his works.

Does the average Mason voting for or against ritual changes at the yearly Grand Lodge Communication know of the origins of the Bible and its connection to Freemasonry, or are they superimposing their personal religious convictions onto the Craft? Do they vote with a logical mind, or are they voting with their heart, believing that Freemasonry is a religion because all they have ever heard is the words "Holy Bible" in Lodge? Are they voting for the good of Freemasonry and their grand lodge in particular? How many vote of out a prejudicial feeling that changing the wording is to allow Muslims to take over, forgetting that Islam is the largest practiced religion in the world and that the book of Moral Law placed upon the altar changes from Lodge to Lodge in many jurisdictions.

Depending on the faiths of the Brethren present, or the Master in the East, this could include a Worshipful Master who is of the Islamic faith. Some Brethren have publically stated due to the attack terrorist attacks on 9/11 that Islam is an evil religion and that Muslims should not be Freemasons as all. This is a prejudicial thought and statement, one that has no place in the Masonic Fraternity. It is what is expressed by Brethren about ritual language labeling a Holy Book used in Masonic Lodges that they themselves do not understand the basis of the intent, or history of the usage of the word Bible in many cases, that leads to discriminatory actions. Using a set of words to define a specific faith when better words more suited to encompass all faiths, specifically in consideration that a lodge is not a church, is an act of discrimination.

Is it intentional? I do not believe so, and nor should anyone else. After all, we are all Masons. However, as society forms its opinions based more on belief that substantiated fact, instead of conducting research without bias, we cannot expect the Masonic fraternity, a microcosm of society, to act much differently. We should hope Masons would, but all are imperfect. If a Mason does not study in full, he is simply a profane minded member of the Fraternity than actually improving himself in masonry.

Will the fraternal membership fracture? History shows it has been done in the past. If one looks at the spurious masonic epidemic in the United States, there are fractures amongst the spurious Masons already, numbering more than 400. These Grand Lodges are already operating within the Masonic territories of regular Grand Lodges. Each Grand Lodge formed is usually from an expelled Mason from a regular masonic jurisdiction who was displeased at how the fraternity was conducting itself, or from a person who was never regularly made a mason, unaccepting that Freemasonry should be regulated. From their lack of education or acceptance of masonic standards, they removed themselves from their spurious organization to simply form another in their vision. One such removal from a prior to begin anew recently took place in Texas.

On May 24, 2014, a person by the name of Andre Jones was installed as the new Grand Master of H.B. Turner Grand Lodge, a newly organized grand lodge by a reported 208 members departing from another spurious grand lodge, the U.M.W. Scottish Rite Grand Lodge in Texas. According to research conducted by John Hairston, a member of J.C. Logan Lodge No. 53 of the Prince Hall Grand Lodge of Washington, who operates *The Quill and The Sword* blog, reported and proved that this young man at the age of 24 was successful at building membership in his previous lodge as its worshipful master, was casted out by the leaders of the grand lodge, and motivated 208 men and woman to leave the former and join his new grand lodge. Here is a picture of Andre Jones, bottom center, at his installation:

What would cause a young man to believe confidently that he could form a new grand lodge? The father of spurious Freemasonry, John G. Jones. This historical figure alone does not alone perpetuate this seemingly unbreakable cycle spurning new spurious grand lodges every day, but he is the foundation. It is the temporarily successful actions of others, of which the initial success and not the failures are reported to others, given in a charismatic and confident manner that provides the inspiration. In August of 2013, a man by the name of Rick Wells from Austin, Texas fraudulently gained membership in an English Lodge of the United Grand Lodge of England, Internet Lodge No. 9659. After being elected to membership, Rick Wells visited a Lodge in Cambridge, Massachusetts, presented his letter of good standing, and gained legal access to the lodge. He subsequently posted the picture on social media and those knowing him to be of a spurious lodge, questioned his membership and reported him to the lodge.

He presented to the membership of Internet Lodge No. 9659 that he was a Past Master of Roger Hughes Lodge No. 624 in Austin, Texas, subordinate to the Prince Hall Grand Lodge of Texas, having been initiated on April 4, 2003, passed on June 11, 2004 and raised on May 27, 2005. It was later discovered that he was a spurious mason who had never held membership at any time in Roger Hughes Lodge No. 624, or any other regularly constituted Lodge of Masons. He initially presented to the lodge with his petition numerous photos of him in masonic attire and a fraudulent letter from his lodge secretary, who doesn't exist. On January 3, 2014, the Prince Hall Grand Lodge of Texas wrote to the United Grand Lodge of England confirming that the letter of good standing given to the Lodge as proof of good financial standing by Wells, was a forgery. Accordingly, on January 11, 2014, Rick Wells was expelled under Rule 181 of the Book of Constitutions, for bringing the name of Internet Lodge No. 9659 into disrepute by fraudulently attempting to gain admission into the United Grand Lodge of England. The damage had been done. Rick Wells appeared in a Harvard Lodge in Cambridge, Massachusetts wearing English regalia, the day after he received his clearance letter and posted the picture all over the internet. The incident was heard around the masonic world.

In an announcement that was issued in what was perhaps was a spurious grand lodge news leaflet, it stated that on "January 6, 2014, members of Aries Lodge No. 4 and Hosea Lodge No. 7, working under the Most Worshipful John G. Jones Grand Lodge of California A.F.&A.M., traveled to Irvine, California to receive the degrees of the ancient Primitive Rite of Memphis Misraim, conferred upon them by Brother Rick Wells 33°/95° who is a member of the United Grand Lodge of England and Abraham Grand Lodge A.F.&A.M. of Texas.

Rick Wells is then seen on the internet presenting pictures proving his acceptance by mainstream Shriners in Austin, Texas, allowing the mainstream Shriners to presume he may be a Prince Hall Shriner as the Grand Lodge of Texas has amity with the Prince Hall Grand Lodge of Texas. The Potentate, presuming he is taking an innocent photo that is in assistance to the representation of Freemasonry and Shriners in particular, happily agrees to the photo, unsuspecting that a Mason and Shriner would commit fraud.

Rick Wells, presenting his letter and his soon received certificate of membership from the United Grand Lodge of England, issued before the meeting that could expel him and prevent him from receiving it, gathered support that he was indeed a legitimate Mason and to his followers, established in their minds that the spurious grand lodge that he was factually a member of was recognized as a Masonic one by the United Grand Lodge of England. "We are legitimate," is what he boasts to those of his jurisdictions membership. He used fraud to build his credibility in the eyes of his spurious group that no person outside of his trust could refute. Members of the Lodge cannot release private lodge information that all have access to in a means to prove this person a fraud.

It has been suggested by some witnessing this debacle unfold and the continued belief that Rick Wells and Weston Jarvis are being truthful about being members of the United Grand Lodge of England by those around them, that cognitive dissonance, a theory that suggests that we have an inner drive to hold all our attitudes and beliefs in harmony and avoid disharmony, allows this continual behavior to exist without confrontation by others within their circle.

To further show the perpetuation of fraud, a man by the name of Weston Jarvis would enlist the assistance of Rick Wells' clearance letter, copied and pasted his name upon the letter, then issued a public statement that he had now joined Internet Lodge No. 9659. I was sent as proof by Weston Jarvis in a conversation where he introduced himself as a member of my lodge, and challenged me to contact my lodge's secretary of Internet Lodge No. 9659 if I did not believe him. This clearance certificate, given to members as proof of good financial standing, is similar to that given by the U.S. Grand Lodges' secretary to a member who is going to travel to a foreign jurisdiction. The problem with the certificate sent to me was that the membership secretary John Dutchman-Smith does not issue these letters, the lodge secretary does which is Alan Breward. As I suspected, Weston had copied and pasted his name on the previous certificate given to Rick Wells, which was fraudulently obtained. The lodges' hard working membership secretary has had to continually deny petitions for membership due to the fraud committed by both Rick Wells, and now Weston Jarvis. Here is a copy of the letter sent to me as proof of Jarvis' membership:

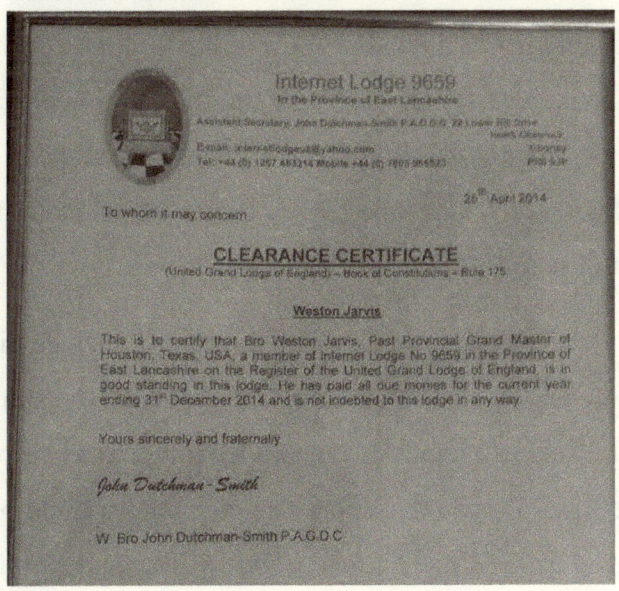

The Secretary of Internet Lodge issued a public stating refuting this letter, which is a fraudulent letter. The secretary stated:

> "As the current secretary of the Internet Lodge No. 9659, I can confirm that Mr. Weston is NOT a member of the Lodge AND never has been.
>
> Regards,
>
> S&F,
>
> Alan Breward PProvGSuptWks (Worcs)"

Even in the face of an official statement issued by the lodge, members loyal to Weston Jarvis simply dismiss the statement as fraud. Not long after this statement was released, Weston Jarvis, and Rick Wells were at the installation of Andre Jones. This simply substantiates the intent of both Rick Wells and Weston Jarvis.

A reasonable person would have to conclude that the only reason Rick Wells sought to fraudulently gain membership in a regularly constituted lodge was to prove to the less informed that spurious grand lodges could be accepted by the United Grand Lodge of England, despite what so many Prince Hall Masons have stated to these individuals time and time again. With the members of the English Lodge forbidden to openly share information to refute his claim, which he knew, regular masons were left powerless to refute his claims beyond words. The goal of Wells and Jarvis is obvious. Titles of grandeur and money.

There is no desire of membership into an honorable fraternity being displayed by the actions of these persons. They have simply committed fraud in what can be deduced to as a pyramid scheme no different than the average criminal. Displaying to the public the goodness of their organization by performing the same charities as church's and other community groups such as fish fry's, scholarship fundraisers and so forth, which are the same tactics used in money laundering schemes.

Why do this? Why continually form new spurious grand lodges? Is it dissatisfaction with the operating procedures and leadership? Maybe. Sometimes. But most often, it comes down to money. In Illinois, there are currently 78 spurious Grand Lodges listed by both the Phylaxis Society, Masonicinfo.com, and Paul Bessel from Bessel.org combined. The Phylaxis society tracks these organizations when reported and pursues them through investigating their tax reports. These organizations, filing as 501c3 nonprofit charitable organizations file form 990 with their filings, and this is where the net profits are documented. The average spurious grand lodge in Illinois had a gross profit of $45,000 a year in 2011. As a stand along grand lodge, that number is pretty insignificant. Collectively, this number balloons to a gross profit of $3,510,000.00 a year.

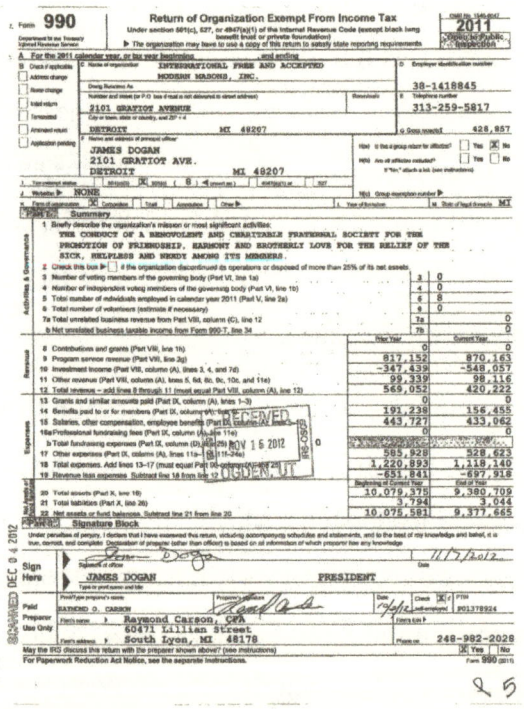

This form 990 shown here is from the 2011 tax year of the International Free and Accepted Modern Masons signed by James O. Dogan, which shown earlier in this book to be spurious, had $422,000.00 in revenue, paid in salaries $433,062.00 to his Board of Directors consisting of less than six people, which several are related.

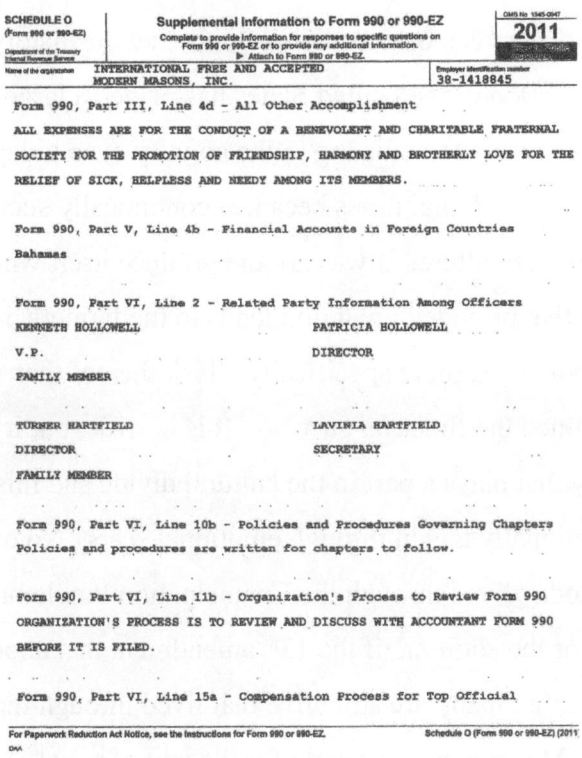

This is money made in the name of Freemasonry, which it uses the fraternity's history to substantiate who they are, to which organizations commit assault and battery on men who can never receive the rights and benefits of traditional Freemasonry. So, it seems it really comes down to the money. Weston Jarvis reportedly earns $500.00 per person whom he knights a member of the Memphis Misraim, to which he has no authority to perform either.

There can be no rational doubt that the history of the formation of the United States has played a large part of the ethnic isolation existing in the country even today. America in colonial times became economically successful through agriculture. It was not the produce itself when traded that provided great dividends to the farmers, it was the labor costs, more specifically a lack thereof that constituted the financial success. It is horrific, but it is history that plays a part in the cultural divide and mistrust, generationally taught through emotional scars. No one alive today lived through the Emancipation Proclamation of 1863, or the addition of the 13th amendment that abolished slavery, but many are still alive that lived through the Civil Rights Movement that fought for the end of racial segregation and for equality supported by the law. The hatred of the past is taught as no human is born hating another due to skin color, this is taught. These feelings generate convictions that are acted upon when making decision relative to the interaction with another ethnicity.

Cultural ideologies displayed publically in society play a significant role in the mistrust that is exemplified in the microcosm of the same society masonic lodges reside within. Prejudice of all kinds. Race, sexual preference, religion, all produced by associative knowledge, based on emotions, and in the respect of the treatment of races and sexual preference, out of context used biblical texts.

One has to ask themselves, is fighting against ideas of good Brethren based upon feelings and interpretations of religious dogma at the imperfect hands of man rather than facts worth continuing down a path that will lead to eventually disdain and separation of Freemasons, more spurious Grand Lodges, or an eventual dissolve of the Masonic Fraternity as it exists today? To understand how this current culture of confliction of ideas have come to exist, and how it has assisted in the perpetuation of spurious Freemasonry, particularly in the United States, it is necessary to explore and analyze the roots of the current prejudicial mindset and discriminatory practices still prevalent in the Fraternity that through the age of the Internet, has spilled into the public for Freemasons to either answer too and correct, or continue to be part of the problem.

What is a culture? Dr. Fred E. Jandt, currently Dean of the Palm Desert Campus and Professor of Communication at California State University, best known for his book *Win-Win Negotiating*, states that culture is defined as a "community or population sufficiently large enough to be self-sustaining, that is, large enough to produce new generations of members without relying on outside people."[xliv] American culture, as diverse as it has become, divided into numerous subcultures, continues to have a noticeable divide between whites and minorities. Minorities consist of non-white ethnicities. Woman and the LGBT community are even more of a minority than those classified by race compared to the white majority. The effects of the history of the United States in regard to social equality predicated on the exterior representation of an individual have repercussions both acted out purposefully, and subconsciously, in one's decisions made in the interacting with another beyond their cultural security. The emotional scars endured by Blacks and their depiction of whites can be symbolically presented as this:

Or this:

Adversely, a culturally isolated Caucasian may subconsciously perceive an African-American as this, a picture of Huey Newton, organizer of the Black Panther Party, who became restless with the disenfranchised and abused African-American by racists in America:

Mass generalizations have no place in the masonic fraternity. What is practiced in Lodge will reveal themselves in the public. As Freemasons learn by symbols, illustrating meanings to us in a means to teach, inspire, and remind us of our obligations, so are Freemasons symbolic to humanity for the same purpose. Freemasons are to exhibit Light, meaning moral truths exemplified by actions, that serves to guide humanity to a better place.

Remember, membership has already dwindled from 3 million in the United States in 1960, to half that number in 2014. Can we not allow our convictions to be challenged in the spirit of Brotherly Love, and practice temperance in our listening to a Brother's concerns to perpetuate our existence? How can one choose not to apply masonic education in its entirety to solve a masonic problem? For if all we do is form lines against another based on what we feel, rather than listening and seeing information substantiated by facts, and what is masonically realistic, we will continue to repeat that attitudes of the past that have led to separation instead of uniting, and regression instead of moral progression.

Chapter 4
An Extension of the Olive Branch

From symbolical masonic darkness to light, enlightenment through the exploration of a man's most inner conceptions weighed against timeless philosophy hidden away in ritual and symbolism, Brotherly Love by way of a tie stronger than any human hands can impose, the Fraternity of Freemasons are to represent the universality of Freemasonry under the Fatherhood of God. Are these the precepts of the most ancient and honorable fraternity ever to exist? I would presume that all members of the Fraternity would answer in the affirmative to this question as these components greatly contribute in differentiating the Fraternity of Freemasons from any other fraternal order in existence. Charity and benevolence is often misunderstood and misapplied in its masonic meaning as the fraternity lost its identity in the last half of the 20th century attempting to fulfill the need of creating a social environment to facilitate comradery, rather than to be the institution of higher philosophical instruction and applicable morality. It is this change of culture that made Albert Pike's words of 1875, "Prince Hall lodge was as regular a Lodge as any lodge created by competent authority," gets pushed by the wayside.

The advancement of the recognition of the Prince Hall Grand Lodges began on June 2, 1988 when Grand Master Richard A. Claytor of the Prince Hall Grand Lodge of Massachusetts sent a letter to the United Grand Lodge of England stating in part that he was writing on behalf of some "300,000 Prince Hall Masons, 42 jurisdictions, 5000 Lodges, who trace their lineage to a Charter issued African Lodge # 459, on September 29, 1784, by the Grand Masters Command and signed by R. Holt, D.G.M., and witnessed by WM. White, GS: - Our legality has been proven many times over he stated and yet we are denied the full rights of Masonry; we have the only charter issued from the Mother Grand Lodge to this country and we are still not recognized as Masons"[xlv] and closed by stating "I humbly ask that you consider placing Prince Hall Masonry in your directory of free Masons," giving light to the cultural darkness existing in Freemasonry in the United States. This would not be the first attempt at establishing amity between the U.S. and the Prince Hall Grand Lodges. A Master Mason learns through his ritual progressions that Freemasonry is a morally progressive society. What exactly does this mean though, the words "morally progressive?"

The definition of moral states, "Arising from conscience or the sense of right and wrong." To progress means to advance beyond one certain state of place or being, too another. So to cause an advancement in morality, to be morally progressive, one would have to continually pursue an elevation or advancement in both understanding and judging the current state of morality, as it relates to humanity, and one would have to constantly seek how to improve this condition. The imperfections of the human condition provides ample opportunity to consider such room for improvements and at one time, the Masonic Fraternity led mankind in this task, was respected for it, and was looked too for guidance.

The anti-masonic movement in the United States was a major blow to the status once held by the Fraternity of Freemasons, morally progressive men who were "square-dealing." The golden age of fraternities would be the last of the biggest noted public effect of Freemasonry on society, benefit societies embodying the practices and general appearance of the masonic fraternity but with financial security benefits the masonic fraternity did not then, nor now, engage in or service to their members. Two World Wars and several conflicts later, membership is half of what it was, but why? Some will say that now is the time for active recruitment of members, as if becoming a Mason is some kind of military enlistment and we simply need to replenish the ranks for those that have simply left, or those that have answered the call of the Grand Architect of the Universe to come home. Others will say we should quietly do what we have been doing because that is what we have always done. Well here is a newsflash, the good the Fraternity of regular Freemasons and its appendant bodies continue to do are not even close to being as well known as the mistakes of our Brethren, and the continual spreading of misconceptions unchecked in the new technological age. A chance for the display of greatness in the arena of moral progression, and the opportunity for it to be captured publically and shared around the world in a second had presented itself.

At the Supreme Council, 33°, S.J., U.S.A. 2013 Biennial Session, Sovereign Grand Commander of the Southern Jurisdiction, Illustrious Ronald A. Seale, 33°, announced that the Southern Jurisdiction of the Scottish Rite of the United States has extended formal recognition to both the Northern and Southern Scottish Rite Prince Hall Affiliated Jurisdictions. Illustrious John William

McNaughton, 33°, Sovereign Grand Commander of the Northern Masonic Jurisdiction, extended the same formal recognition to the Southern Jurisdiction of the Scottish Rite, Prince Hall Affiliated. The Northern Masonic Jurisdictions, which composes the northeast 15 states of the country, has had mutual recognition since 1995. As to be expected, once the news of the formal recognition extended to the Southern Jurisdiction of the Scottish Rite, Prince Hall Affiliated, by both the Southern and Northern Masonic Jurisdictions, comments for and against presented themselves. The process of the formal recognition being extended, becoming mutual, was then left to Illustrious Deary Vaughn, 33°, the Sovereign Grand Commander of the Southern Jurisdiction of the Scottish Rite, Prince Hall Affiliated, and the members of Southern Jurisdiction to consider at their annual session in mid-October in North Carolina of 2013. The Prince Hall Grand Lodge of Arkansas members would be inspired to propose something similar. A new resolution was sent out to the world by the Prince Hall Grand Lodge of Arkansas to be considered, a new olive branch to test the bounds of Fraternal Brotherhood and those precepts we are to represent, once again.[xlvi]

On February 22, 2014, the Most Worshipful Prince Hall Grand Lodge of Arkansas passed a resolution stating:

> "Be it resolved, that it shall be the policy of the M.W. Prince Hall Grand Lodge of Arkansas to recognize and offer into fraternal relations with any all Grand Lodges which (1) hold a seat in the Conference of Grand Masters of North America, Inc., and (2) have entered into an agreement, treaty, or compact, of recognition with the M.W. Prince Hall Grand Lodge who is a member of the Conference of Grand Masters of Prince Hall Masons, Inc. in their respective state…"

Before dissecting the pros and cons of this resolution, let us explore what amity is and how a masonic jurisdiction can be eligible for the extension of recognition from one Grand Lodge to another, the history of the attempts, both the failures and successes, and where Grand Lodges in the United States stand today in terms of amity. From there, we will explore how conceivable any action on this resolution may be by U.S. Grand Lodges.

Amity is by definition a "mutual understanding and a peaceful relationship, especially between nations." Masonically, amity is a recognition compact between two masonic grand Lodges who deem the other as conforming to the same standards of regularity, and agree that mutual recognition would be in the best interest of Freemasonry and for the members of their Grand Lodges in particular. The standards of regularity that makes a Grand Lodge deemed regular is decided by each Grand Lodge as all Grand Lodges are sovereign.

In the United States, Grand Lodges belonging to the Conference of Grand Masters of North America deem the standards a Grand Lodge must adhere to in order to be recommended for recognition are: "Legitimacy of Origin," meaning the Grand Lodge can produce factual evidence that the lodges that organized it were previously chartered by an existing regular Grand Lodge conforming to the same standards, and this process repeated back into time until it finds its beginnings at the first organized speculative Grand Lodge in England, the moderns, or the third Grand Lodge, the ancients, both of which formed the United Grand Lodge of England today, in existence since 1813, the Grand Lodge of Scotland, or the Grand Lodge of Ireland. "Exclusive Territorial Jurisdiction, except by mutual consent and/or treaty." This means a Grand Lodge cannot be organized within a state boundary where a previous Grand Lodge has already been established without a mutual agreement. 18 Grand Lodges in the United States are without recognition and publically, the U.S. Grand Lodges have cited this clause as a reason recognition does not exist. Finally, "Adherence to the Ancient Landmarks – specifically, a Belief in God, the Volume of Sacred Law as an indispensable part of the Furniture of the Lodge, and the prohibition of the discussion of politics and religion." This last necessity shows adherence to the tradition established by the ancient charges of the Craft noted in the Constitution of James Anderson written in 1723, which were inspired by many of the Masonic Manuscripts found starting with the Regius Manuscripts circa 1390. The Prince Hall Conference of Grand Master's standards for recognition are basically similar and can be found in details made available by the Phylaxis Society Website or Magazine.

Amity, otherwise known commonly as a compact of recognition, was originally known as establishing 'constant correspondence,' and is first noted in 1740. According to John Belton, an English Freemason and author of the book The English Masonic Union of 1813, in Scotland on December 1, 1740, the Right Honorable Thomas, Earl of Strathmore and Kinghorn, was elected Grand Master and at the meeting "It was proposed, and unanimously agreed to, that a correspondence should be opened between the Grand Lodge of Scotland and the Grand Lodge of England." The Grand Master, having been Grand Master of the Grand Lodge of England, the ancients, finding himself later in the elected position of the Grand Master of Scotland, desired to be able to communicate freely and visit with his former constitution without incident and thus, the establishment of amity was necessary for him to "travel in foreign countries, work, and receive a master's wage." This same form of amity was eventually established between the Grand Lodge of Ireland and the Ancients as well, effectively leaving the premier Grand Lodge of England alone on a Masonic island which may have politically motivated the Union of 1813, for the best interest of the Fraternity. African Lodge No. 459, having been regularly chartered in 1784 by the Grand Lodge of England, the Moderns, and declaring its independence as a Grand Lodge in 1808, was not yet in the equation of amity, but it would be soon.

In 1897, two Black Masons wrote to the Grand Lodge of Washington asking that a way be found so that they might visit a subordinate lodge of that jurisdiction. An investigation committee consisting of Thomas M. Reed,

James E. Edminston and William H. Upton, two of them Past Grand Masters of the Grand Lodge of Washington, was formed to investigate the request and found the Prince Hall Grand Lodge of Washington to be "Just, Regular, and legitimate." What happened next during a time where slavery was not yet abolished was inevitable. More than seventeen Grand Lodges holding amity with the Grand Lodge of Washington rescinded recognition and the following year, to make amends with other Grand Lodges, the Grand Lodge of Washington rescinded recognition of the Prince Hall Grand Lodge of Washington. The decision to rescind recognition was not due to a logical reason, but of a culturally relative reason. One could effectively hide behind the Exclusive Territory Doctrine, but a more common sense reason would be the misapplied understanding of the qualifications for one to be made a Mason: Freeborn, of good report, and well recommended. Even in conversation today Brethren hold that they are comfortable making men Masons of any ethnicity except Blacks as they are not Freeborn, descendent in the United States from slaves. Freeborn is an allegorical term, not one to be taken literally. John S. Nagy, author of the book series *Building Better Builders Series of Uncommon*

Masonic Education books goes into this terminology in greater depth. But, I digress.

In 1947, the Grand Lodge of Massachusetts efforted the same notion of recognition and was met with negative influence to rescind it after many U.S. Grand Lodges severed their masonic relationship with them. Wisconsin, North Dakota, and Connecticut Grand Lodges built momentum that finally ended in a resolve that Prince Hall Grand Lodges are undeniably regular and in the spirit of Freemasonry should be recognized. Connecticut became the first grand lodge to officially recognize the Prince Hall Grand Lodge of Massachusetts, formally African Grand Lodge, in 1989 with the Grand Lodge of Colorado to immediately follow. To date, many Grand Lodges in the international masonic community and all but nine U.S. Grand Lodges have formal recognition with the Prince Hall Grand Lodges.

To be clear, it is not without effort that some of the remaining nine Grand Lodges within the United States have proposed recognition. In May of 2010, according to Brother Christopher Hodapp's blog, R.W. Brother Seth L. Rothstein, P.D.D.G.M., Solomon Lodge No. 20, Brother Simon D. Rothstein, Solomon Lodge No. 20, and Brother

Fitzhugh K. Powell, Solomon Lodge No. 20, put forth a motion to extend recognition to The Most Worshipful Union Grand Lodge of The Most Ancient and Honorable Fraternity of Free and Accepted Masons of the State of Florida, Belize, Central America and Jurisdiction, which had already passed a resolution many years earlier to recognize the Florida Grand Lodge. The Jurisprudence Committee of the Grand Lodge of Florida recommended rejection of this motion and it failed. In February of 2010, "The Grand Lodge of Louisiana, F&AM determined that "technicalities" in the filing of the Prince Hall (PHA) recognition resolution prevented it from being accepted for debate and a proper vote." The Prince Hall Grand Lode of Georgia issued the same resolution that the Prince Hall Grand Lodge of Arkansas has just issued, but with no success. This was to be expected in Georgia where the constitution read as of 2009 that a "non-white" could not be made a mason which was the foundation of the charges of unmasonic conduct by two lodges in Georgia upon Gate City Lodge No. 2 raising an African-American to the Degree of Master Mason. In West Virginia, Past Grand Master Frank Hass and a Judge in West Virginia, was expelled from the Grand Lodge of West Virginia without a Masonic Trial for his attempt to establish amity with the

Prince Hall Grand Lodge of West Virginia. The Grand Lodge of Ohio attempted to accommodate Hass by remaking him a Master Mason, but this action with good intentions and resulted in the withdrawal of recognition of Ohio by West Virginia. Still today, Frank Hass is an expelled Mason for acting in the best interest of Freemasonry.

"Upon occasion masons must do that which is right because it is right and must not be intimidated by those with other less noble agendas." -- Ken W. Aldridge, Grand Secretary, Grand Lodge of Quebec, letter to UGLE, 1991-07-23

On a trip to Colorado Springs, Colorado in February of 2014, which was facilitated by Brother Cliff Porter, author of the *Secret Psychology of Freemasonry* and *A Traditional Observance Lodge*, I was honored to attend a Prince Hall Lodge, Pike's Peak Lodge No. 5, before my presentation at the Valley of Southern Colorado the following day. What an incredible Masonic experience! I was almost in cultural shock as I have not seen in the Midwest on a large scale what I am accustomed to seeing in the North East Masonic states, inter-visitation so wide spread and lodges so diverse that I was left unsure, aside from the Grand Officers, who were members of the Prince Hall Grand Lodge of Colorado, and who were members of the Grand Lodge of Colorado. The Lodges in which I hold membership, and a few others in Illinois, are very ethnically diverse and beaming with Brotherly Love, but it is not the norm and inter-visitation aside from Grand Lodge Officers at Grand Lodge, is uncommon. I was emotionally moved to see such nonexistent boundaries of Brotherly Love. I stood there thinking, "I wonder if those without inter-visitation or recognition know what they are missing?"

In common practice, recognition is requested, as Brother Ed King from Maine states on his Masonic Info Website, in this order: "A senior Masonic organization (Grand Lodge) would receive a request from another more junior Grand Lodge that it be recognized as well - and that Masonic courtesies be extended so that brethren might visit between their respective lodges." This is the practice as I have known it to be as well. Having said that and returning to addressing the resolution by the Prince Hall Grand Lodge of Arkansas, there is no reason that a Grand Lodge currently in amity with a Prince Hall Grand Lodge should not enter into amity with the Prince Hall Grand Lodge of

Arkansas. None. This Grand Lodge seeks to be recognized by the very fact of their statement in the final paragraph of the resolution, "…recognize and offer into fraternal relations…" This Grand Lodge was formed according to the standards of recognition by the COGMNA. There is a potential problem for amity which should not be a problem, but it can be used as a scapegoat.

In contrast to this great opportunity of extending recognition between existing regular grand lodges, spurious grand lodges are attempting to accomplish this same feat of recognition, providing for their members to freely travel amongst spurious grand lodge jurisdictions. This new phenomenon may potentially create a problem of great magnitudes to which United States Freemasonry may be ill prepared for currently, for it is nothing they have seen in the past.

Spurious Grand Lodges such as those consisting of the Regular Grand Lodge of Illinois have entered into mutual recognition compacts with other termed "regular" grand lodges of other states. The Regular Grand Lodge of Virginia entered into such a compact with the National Phoenician Grand Lodge of Lebanon.

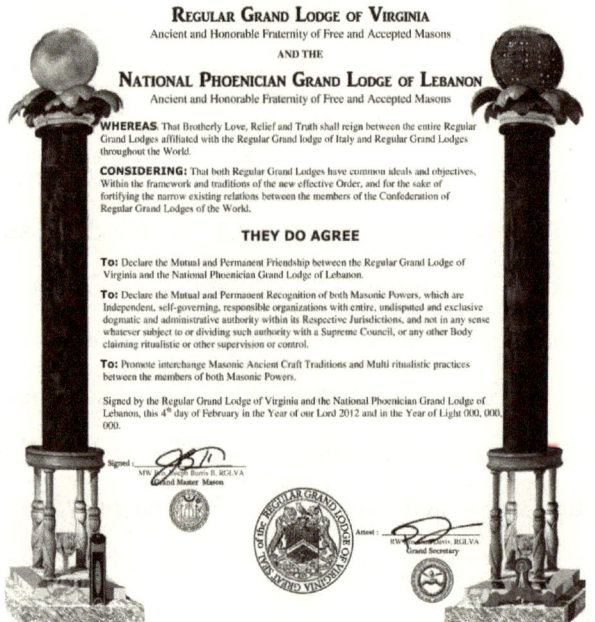

These mutual recognition compacts, between spurious grand lodges in the United States, and between spurious foreign grand lodges, are becoming the norm amongst spurious Freemasonry. Westin Jarvis, mentioned earlier in this book, has begun to give lectures about the importance of International Masonic Fellowship.

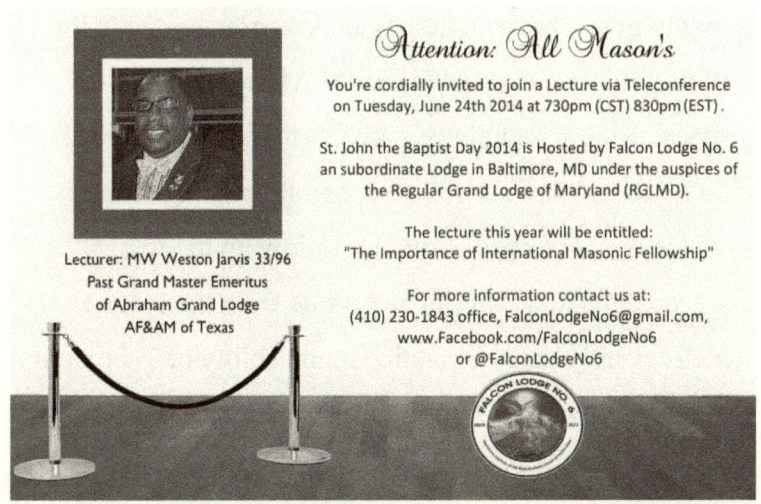

The United Grand Lodge of England, in remaining neutral amongst the Grand Lodges in the United States and the Prince Hall Grand Lodges, both of which are regular Grand Lodges, will not recognize a junior Grand Lodge sharing a territory with the senior Grand Lodge unless they are both in amity. Without recognition being established between the Arkansas Grand Lodges first, will other Grand Lodges already having amity sidestep the Grand Lodge of Arkansas and agree to accommodate the Prince Hall Grand Lodge anyway? Maybe not. There are members of the Grand Lodge of Arkansas who desire recognition to be established, but the culture is such that receiving a majority vote on a proposal may not be probable. Personally, I was going to give a presentation in an Arkansas Lodge in the Fall of 2013, but in speaking to the Master who had no problem with my ethnicity asked, "How dark of a Black man I was as there are still less than favorable attitudes towards Blacks there." I did not follow up to the engagement and let it pass by. Aside from the culture which severely lacks a practice in the ability of intercultural communication, U.S. Grand Lodges may refuse to accommodate the Prince Hall Grand Lodge of Arkansas' request in an attempt to support Arkansas' practice of the Exclusive Territory Doctrine.

The question becomes, "Who will push the agenda for the betterment of the Fraternity?" There are tangible negative effects of a lack of recognition established between the last 18 Grand Lodges in the southern part of the United States. From the perception of Masons outside of the United States, newly made Master Masons, and the public in general, the question is continually asked why there are separate Grand Lodges, one predominately Black and the other predominantly White. This would be easy to answer without fear of further questioning if one could say, "Out of the dark history of the United States that created a need for a separate Grand Lodge of Masons for Blacks, we remain separate not due to racism, but of maintaining traditional history." We cannot say that now in truth because the lack of recognition in the south negates the answer being fully credible. We have to answer with a hyphen on the end of the statement, ready to further explain without further exploring and showing a negative reality of the situation relative to cultural perception.

So the question becomes again, who will do what is right by foregoing the fear of the eventual initial negative backlash? Are we afraid of our Grand Lodges losing recognition based on another Grand Lodges' refusal to share their territory like 40 other states have? Merging Grand Lodges would solve the problem, but that is not a realistic option as it took 62 years for the two Grand Lodges of England to unite, and questions deriving from ethnicities was not in the cultural equation. Will members of both U.S. and Prince Hall Grand Lodges that are without amity of one another put aside their emotional resentments resulting from America's dark past? I do not know. It is difficult to move forward if one is constantly looking in the past, effectively chasing their tail instead of progressing, looking for apologies or blame.

I have been faced with comments by both U.S. Grand Lodge and Prince Hall Masons regarding the negatives of the other. At one lecture I gave on how we can understand the applicability of masonic symbolism in the pursuit of moral progression, a Brother referred to White Masons as "The oppressor," and told me I should be lecturing the white masons instead of them. My father in the audience promptly stood and informed the Brother that this was the first predominately African-American audience I had given this presentation. He sat back down.

As noted in my first book, *Freemasonry in Black and White*, A Mason said Blacks cannot be Masons as they are born of slaves. These mindsets are born of minds in darkness, one born of emotional scars and the other with a lack of masonic insight. These are terrible statements, but are repeated more than one would ever like to imagine. But, we can change this. It is simply a choice by each man to do what is right because it is morally the right thing to do without fear of repercussions such as losing a vote to move forward in the officer line at lodge. We are Freemasons.

Throughout history, we have been rebellious of immoral laws and practices since the age of Enlightenment, and through until now. Or, have we lost the nerve? Have we allowed ourselves to be ushered into the rear of society and by a refusal or because of complacency not acted, encouraged the profane to show us what it means to take a stand on moral principles. I say no. We are to be the example by virtue of our conduct that enlightens others into a better humane existence. We do what is right when no one is looking and whether we are to be held accountable by the laws of man or not. We are bound to each other and the moral law by a tie, stronger than human hands can impose. So I ask, will we now strengthen and expand that circle we find ourselves to be the point within, or will we look the other way and leave the responsibility to act to someone else? I admonish all, please, listen to the whisper of good counsel. And, with truth and justice on our side, pursue what is right to take the action of what is moral.

Chapter 5

A Time to Display Moral Progression

Let us consider what a great moment it was, the electing to extend recognition from one Southern Jurisdiction, to that of the other, being Prince Hall Affiliated, and place into context the meaning of this moment. In 1775, the first African-American was made a Mason under the constitution of the Grand Lodge of Ireland. Why Ireland one asks? America was not the United States as of yet and slavery was a financially profitable industry. Having an African-American man, even if he were a free man, sitting beside a white man in a Masonic Lodge at that time would not have happened. A lodge was a place where men met on the level, and a slave owner was not going to be placed on the same level as a slave, or anyone mistaken for one. January 1, 1863, President Lincoln ordered the end of slavery in the United States, sealing his endeavor with the passage of the 13th amendment just two years later. Prince Hall Masonry was doing better than the mainstream Grand Lodges through the anti-masonic period. They in fact, thrived. Though free man, Masonic Lodges, the places were men were equal, was still no place for African-Americans in the eyes of mainstream Freemasons. 1964, the passage of the Civil Rights Act ending segregation, concluding in the March on Washington, led by Dr. Martin Luther King Jr. and his famous, "I have A Dream" speech. 100 years past the end of slavery and it will still not be until 1989 that mutual recognition between the Prince Hall Grand Lodge of Massachusetts and the Grand Lodge of Massachusetts would be established, the seeing of one another as Masons, as equals.

    The question any true blue Masons should be asking is, "Why did it take so long?" The answer to this question can be found in the understanding of cultural relativism. In other words, the answer to why Whites for so long did not want or accept African-Americans, and vice-versa, Whites visiting in their lodges, was a consequence of the culture they were immersed in. This also goes for why so many Prince Hall Grand Lodges have recognition with all other Prince Hall Grand Lodges, their mainstream counterpart in 40 states and few others, with rare exceptions. Cultural relevance. It sounds simple, a great divide along racial lines being summed up with two neat little words. It isn't. It is worth a moment to analyze at least at the surface level if we are to gain an in-depth understanding of the imminent ramifications that await our southern states that currently do not have amity with one another. These were questions that had to be asked of the Southern Jurisdiction of the

Scottish Rite, Prince Hall Affiliated, and fortunately were answered in the affirmative with the formal recognition extended back to the mainstream Scottish Rite of the Southern Jurisdiction.

Cultural relativism is defined by Fred E. Jandt, author of *Intercultural Communications*, as the "view that an individual's beliefs and behaviors should only be understood in terms of that person's own culture." For centuries, outside of noble actions of liberated minded men and women, clashing with the mainstream views of racial attitudes towards other various races, America has been a collection of immigrants from varies reaches of the other continents, but not a melting pot. Existing separate but equal isolates cultures and ensures that even one community living next to another will allow their living experiences to be foreign to the other. A popular example of cultural relativism is the show, "WifeSwap," which airs on the cable network *Lifetime*. The website of the show posing the plot saying, "Have you ever wondered whether the grass is greener on the other side of the fence? Two wives discover that it often isn't when they hand over the keys to their homes and literally switch families for two weeks." A married woman from the bright lights high end city of Manhattan, switches places with the wife whose family lives off the Earth. They settle into the others homes and families and the first week, live according the house rules. The next week, the visiting wife applies her rules to the new home. The show very seldom has happy campers. The reason that they clash is because they are accustomed to living a certain way, or in a culture, that is very different than the new one they are placed into. Their life experience is relative to where they have spent their lives.

In Freemasonry, specifically in America, there are two major components that have placed their stamp on Freemasonry, slavery and secrecy. Slavery produced two classes of people, those who were owners and those who were pieces of property. In the minds of those without contextual understanding relative to the 18th and 19th centuries of America and how slavery was a thriving business worth fighting over, hence the Civil War, they listen to stories told by generations past, warped by emotion and the times retold, and are mentally led in directions that can be difficult to maneuver away from, unfortunately. Secrecy has prevented the stories from being scrutinized, and thus left uncheck, woven into times shared learning catechisms and passed down reasons of why is it the "way it's always been." Trust in your mentor's words, hearing the same horrid stories of how "they" are, and it does matter the skin color, the stories sound just as bad relative to who is telling and who is listening.

The Southern Jurisdiction of the Scottish Rite, Prince Hall Affiliated accepted and making the recognition mutual was another great milestone in the exemplification to the world that Freemasonry is truly a universal brotherhood and the Fatherhood of God. Imagine if the vote had not passed. The noise that would have come in the days following from those who adorn separate but equal because they believe it is more peaceful. This is where the question of whether the practice by regular Masons, a universal brotherhood, one not inhibited by the societal embrace of racial separation of black and white, will truly meet the road. A question to be asked for the future is how will the members of Mainstream and Prince Hall Grand Lodges, who have not had an amity agreement, feel as those who dare sit in a stated Valley meeting as the only White, or the only African-American Scottish Rite Mason, for the first time? Will members be "overly politically correct," fearing that they might accidentally say the wrong thing because the cultures have never crossed unguarded before? Will there be the stares, or members turning around at the door because they hear someone from the "other side" has shown up to attend a meeting? As awful as all this sounds, this will go through some minds, if not voiced privately, amongst members. It is human nature and it is absolutely nothing to be worried about. The worry at the time was realized as the Grand Lodges who could have possibly felt their exclusive territorial jurisdiction would be undermined was placed at ease as the compact of the Scottish Rites still do not allow Masons whose jurisdictions are not in amity with a foreign jurisdiction of the same territory, to visit the Valleys of the foreign jurisdictions.

Brother Ralph McNeal Jr., a Prince Hall Mason, when asked how the Grand Lodges that do not have amity, if they will feel pressured to establish it, or will Grand Lodges simply issue an edict preventing their members to visit stated, "Those Grand Lodges will present an edict. Some of those SGIGs are PGMs who did not want recognition on their watch. Those same SGIGs are so advisors to their GMs... So with their GMs serving for only one year?? Should be interesting to see the thought process of those coming up thru the line..." He suggested that Grand Masters would issue edicts to prevent their members from sitting in tiled Scottish Rite meetings, a way to exert a control where their members are allowed to visit outside of their Grand Lodge jurisdiction. This suggestion had merit and was correct. The recognition of the Scottish Rite jurisdictions cannot circumvent the authority of the Grand Lodge over its members and whom they can legally visit.

As Brother Johnnie Simpson Jr. states, "My first thought is this will do the route of the Shrine, some GMs forcing loyalty to one or the other, others pulling recognition, but most issuing edicts for their members to leave if a member of a PHA jurisdiction shows up." In the issue between the Grand Lodge of Arkansas and Shriners International most recently, the Grand Lodge of Arkansas withdrew recognition of the Shriners which prevented Craft Lodge Masons from sitting in tiled Shrine meetings. Grand Lodges withdraw recognition from Masonic Bodies and jurisdictions as a means to right what they may perceive as unmasonic, or irregular conduct, by a foreign jurisdiction. So, why would one believe that sitting in a Scottish Rite meeting with a Prince Hall Mason, or vice versa, is irregular or unmasonic? A lack of education or to prove a point of sovereignty?

A mainstream Mason by the name of Joe Seal answered the same question that was asked to Brother Ralph McNeal Jr., and he responded by saying,

"Please clarify this for me, aren't all PHA lodges clandestine, because they don't have a charter from U.G.L.E.? If this is the case, and they went and got a charter tomorrow, we would only be able to recognize MM raised after tomorrow. All raised before this time would be clandestinely made masons! This is not a topic of race acceptance, this is an issue of accepting a man who chose not to follow the rules of our fraternity, but joined a copycat club instead, and now wishes to be recognized as one of us! I say this will tear apart the real fraternity!"

The answer presented is just another display of cultural relativism. One who has not had the need to study or become versed in the history of Prince Hall Masonry would simply be grossly misinformed as to the regularity and mostly recognized masonic jurisdiction. This will be an issue to contend with though with many members. The Exclusive Territorial Doctrine, also known as the American Doctrine, will be called into discussion. To answer this, the

Commission on Information for Recognition said in 1975 that "the doctrine of exclusive territorial jurisdiction means that all the Lodges chartered by a particular Grand Lodge give their loyalty only to that Grand Lodge, but there can be lodges chartered by different Grand Lodges in the same territory."

As it seems with all great undertakings and opportunities presented before man in order to usher in an advancement in society that has less to do with nuts and bolts, and more to do with emotions and lacks of understanding, all should place their trust in the Grand Architect of the Universe. The extension of formal recognition by the Southern Jurisdiction of the Scottish Rite and the return of it by the Southern Jurisdiction of the Scottish Rite, Prince Hall Affiliated in October of 2013 was fantastic.

It has been considered long overdue by many. But as monumental as it was, it brings into clear view those Grand Lodges that will be as of yet without mutual recognition, and the public exploration as to why they are the holdouts in mutual recognition between mainstream and Prince Hall Grand Lodges throughout the rest of the country. They will have to explore their personal understandings of the reasons, constitutionally and morally, why the other 40 states of the Union have found their way to reflect the spirit of brotherhood beyond the shackles of controversial subjects that need not be mentioned in Lodge, that tend to be the factors of cultural separation in the profane world, and they have not.

If we are to exemplify in application what we teach to all our fellows in the Craft, that we are a morally progressive society, then the opportunity is at hand to prove to them, and to all the world, why Freemasons are the leaders of the great moral pushes that promote a better moral world. Now, will there be excuses, or action? Freemasons are ideologically rebellious against immoral ideas that suppress a positive humanity and a progressive speculative spirit. At every opportunity, Masons should seize this moment, and watch the positive ripples reverberate beyond the doors of our lodge and reflect out into the world.

Chapter 6

Tolerance: A True Measure of Compassion

We came here to learn to subdue our earthly passions, to increase our intellect and spiritual awareness, to find Light, or better yet, our spiritual reality. Going one step further, we search for the true understanding of life, our place and purpose in it through the ability to reason.

The realization of the true ability to find reason within the mental and emotional processes of life is the fulcrum between the choices of good and evil, and between right and wrong. This is what we are truly saying when we recite the beginning of our first degree catechism. Sure, the words may differ from one masonic jurisdiction to another, but we all came here to subdue our passions and improve ourselves in Masonry. This process is accomplished through different practices.

    We learn the definitions of the Masonic symbols and from our mentors, we are explained the philosophies. The transformative process of Masonry, the change of one state of conscious and subconscious conviction to a more improved state through the application of spiritual exploration and the understanding of various philosophies, communicated through various symbols within the construct of Masonic ritual to our inner most convictions, start to make themselves realized by the epiphanies we come to have and the changes in our perception of life and those circulating in it. These changes are only possible through study and discussion with those others who have themselves solid understandings of such, and who can provide credible explanations that contributes to self-reflection without bias to the conclusions. How do we measure through self-reflection of how far we have come though?

One of the identifiable measures of how far our passions have been subdued is to pay attention to the depth of our tolerance. Whence did tolerance derive its meaning? What is the difference between possessing tolerance and simply being tolerant? It is that understanding that allows us to measure the tolerance one may possess to calculate how they have identified their vices and superfluities to illustrate to them the direction of education that may need to pursue in the improvement of self.

Tolerance is defined as the "willingness to accept feelings, habits, or beliefs that are different from your own" by the Merriam-Webster Dictionary. In regards to religious tolerance, Daniel Taylor of Christianity Today writes that intolerance became a sin and was developed as a result of the Christian wars of the 16th and 17th century that resulted in mass slaughtering in the name of Christ. He states the answer to the problem was tolerance and that historically then, "was the liberal, secular answer to the inability of conservative religionists to compromise with those who differed from them."

Voltaire, who lived from 1694 until 1778 and who was a Freemason actively involved with the Enlightenment stated that, "Of all religions, the Christian should of course inspire the most tolerance, but until now Christians have been the most intolerant of all men." The word itself came into usage in the 14th century and by the 17th century in France, it meant the same as when it was first used as a "tendency to be free from bigotry or severity in judging others."

Not only is tolerance taught and espoused by Christianity, it is found in all religious dogma in one verse or another. What is interesting is that with examples of tolerance found in all religious texts, the practice of intolerance can be seen in our society by many professed religious leaders from the West and those leaders of other religious faiths, ethnicities, or politics. In an effort to be politically correct, they ACT tolerant, but do not demonstrate a POSSESSION of tolerance. The possession of tolerance and it having depth is different from simply being tolerant.

One's depth of tolerance is predicated on several aspects such as education, philosophical understandings, and the ability to evaluate without influencing the results with the bias of self- conviction. Dialectical thinking, "a form of analytical reasoning that pursues knowledge and truth as long as there are questions and conflicts," is a great asset to have when doing such evaluating of one's measure of tolerance. The absence of bias and attitude of dismissal is essential in the successful use of this method.

An example of the use of this type of investigative academic procedure is the Socratic Method. But as Manzo notes, this method can be easily abused as one asking questions can easily begin their quest as educationally investigative, but without specific and moral direction of the questions, the quest can become misaligned and promote defensive mindsets then resulting in fruitless arguments rather than expanded understanding. The indifference that may result relieves us from gaining the possession of tolerance and may leave us with the resolve of simply tolerating an indifference as to not further spurn more arguing, instead of intellectually or spiritually increasing our understanding of foreign convictions that tends to expands tolerance.

"Let not interest, favour, or prejudice bias your integrity, or influence you to be guilty of a dishonourable action." – William Preston

Cultural Relativism, a topic spoken of earlier in this book, is "a method whereby different societies or cultures are analyzed objectively without using the values of one culture to judge the worth of another," and is another medium to implement a progression in the depth of one's tolerance. In the analysis of another person's character, conviction, or cultural practices of varying natures, our experiences, education, dogma's and so forth, our culture, undoubtedly coerces us to judge in relation to them.

We must, in the interest of the exploration of cultural assimilation for moral improvement to be exemplified to mankind, resist this innate desire to judge with bias. This is not to say that all we objectively attempt to inspect and judge will be of virtuous quality that is beneficial in a positive means of assimilation to our own moral betterment, but if we cannot without bias analyze those who are different from us in whatever respects that are presented, we will deny ourselves even the opportunity to explore if there were qualities that were beneficial to begin with.

The growth of tolerance and resistance to simply be tolerant is a necessity in the advancement of moral progression of humanity with Freemasons being the exemplars. As Albert Pike states in the first Chapter of *Morals and Dogma-*

"The blind force of the people is a force that must be economized, and also managed, as the blind force of steam, lifting the ponderous iron arms and turning the large wheels, is made to bore and rifle the cannon and to weave the most delicate lace. It must be regulated by intellect. Intellect is to the people and the people's force, what the slender needle of the compass is to the ship…"

As many athletic coaches have stated during practices for big games in whatever sport, it is what you do in practice that will ultimately determine your performance on the field. This is not so different than Lodge, which actually is not limited by the walls in which we tile as the Lodge symbolically extends from the East to West, between North and South, from the Earth to the heavens and from the surface to the center. What we exercise in demonstrating the possession of tolerance in Lodge with our brethren and their shared opinions or beliefs is what we intrinsically will demonstrate, and maybe with less awareness, in the public.

I do not doubt that we have heard the sighs from the sideline when a Brother may be expressing a thought, even though he has repeated the same objection time and time again perhaps, as the Brethren have grown tired and desire to end lodge, but I ask, is that a demonstration of tolerance, or simply being tolerant because there are visible repercussions? We must search for why someone is speaking or acting from a particular mindset or with a certain ideology before we can began to rule out the validity of their position. It is this act, this being in "due bounds of mankind and more especially a Brother Mason," that will ultimately vindicate the conviction of our members to be involved with lodge instead of feeling as if they are an outcast, will ultimately give them confidence in contributing to the betterment of the lodge. This act of compassion, this demonstration of tolerance exemplified by the Brethren within the lodge will be exemplified by the same members outside the lodge with an inherent confidence that will leave those of mankind one comes in contact with, inspired.

So, we must ask ourselves, "What came we here to do?" To that, we must add the question of how do we accomplish the answer we profess every time we sit in the West of the Lodge, or listen to the Senior Warden recite to the Master of the Lodge. How do we stem the rising of our blood pressure at the speaking of, or action, of another? How do we bare witness to the measure of our growth in compassion? How do we first learn then teach effectively? How do we right the wrongs of others against us without allowing the wrong to find a seat to scorn beneath our skin? Tolerance.

By understanding how we can develop our tolerance of others in a morally upright manner, we can better implement the tenets of our institution and inspire the world that merit is the title of our privileges and that on us, they have been deservingly bestowed. This will undoubtedly influence those we come into contact with to consider their own moral convictions as they see in us a mirror of their own conduct to be measured. I charge myself often with this large responsibility to improve so I may become a better human being. I fail I small measures each day, but it is only that I try that I find small failures to right my course of thought and conviction. I encourage you to charge yourself with the same responsibility. Together, we can move forward parallel to one another, our differences and similarities working in harmony, expanding our positive effect on one another, and inspiring a better world for those that will endeavor to follow us into the future.

All the analysis and suggestions one can make to give their effort towards a moral progression accomplishes nothing if the suggestions are not analyzed without bias, without prejudice, without preconceived notions. One would be foolish to think that credible evidence substantiated by other corroborating sources will have the impact desired as the words are typed to this page.

All I hope is that just one mason becomes inspired to inspire another which can produce a chain reaction of moral progression that when I look back after I make my progress onto the level of time from whose born no traveler returns, the Supreme Architect will look down upon my work and say good job. We all come to the Craft with our own mistakes, our own errors of judgment that places no one above the other. We meet on the level though, all at the same starting point of our transformative journey. We build upon the plumb, taking note of the Divine Moral Law and the tools we use within due bounds. We part upon the square, leaving all in a place that is morally safe until we shall meet each other again.

Acknowledgements:

To my family, without your support and inspiration, my continued endeavor to effort my contributions to the moral progression of humanity would be difficult. To my friends, Leon Sullivan, Emmett George, Stephen Valle, Tommy Van Buran, Foy Thomas, Shaun Gorley, Jammie Shell, Shaun McPhail, Oscar Alleyne, Mir Omar Ali, Rueben Owens, Alejandro Cabral, Carlton Smith, Robert Johnson and many other Brothers of whom I hold in dear regard, the entire staff at the Living Stones Magazine staff starting with owner Robert Herd, writers and authors John S. Nagy, Anthony Mongelli, Cliff Porter and others, the Brothers of the *Round Table Discussion Group* and the Midnight Freemasons, my Lodge Brothers, Ryan Flynn, whose artwork has graced the cover of this book, thank you. To Ralph McNeal Jr., Ezekiel Bey, and Antoine Lilly, all of the *Phylaxis Society*, thank you for your input. Thank you for your ongoing work in protecting our Fraternity from the epidemic of spurious Freemasonry and providing masonic education in varies facets to our Brethren. It may never be free from fraud, but continued efforts through education can limit it, and hopefully more forcefully stem the tide of its growth.

About the author

Charles M. Harper Sr., M.P.S., is a Master Mason from the State of Illinois who maintains active memberships in two Lodges, Pleiades Lodge No. 478, where is currently Senior Warden and the Masonic Education Officer, and Illumination Lodge No. 5. He serves the Grand Lodge of Ancient Free and Accepted Masons of the State of Illinois as a member of the Illinois Masonic Academic Bowl Committee. He is also a member of Internet Lodge no. 9659 subordinate to the United Grand Lodge of England.

He is a member of the Medinah Shriners. He is a member of Keystone Chapter U.D. R.A.M., Lafayette Chapter No. 2 R.A.M., Chicago Cryptic Council No. 4 R.S.M., and St. Bernard Commandery no. 35 KT, of the York Rite. He is a member of the Valley of Chicago Scottish Rite. He is a member of Illuminati Council No. 495 Allied Masonic Degree Council of the United States of America, where he serves as the Junior Warden and has received the rank of Esquire by the Supreme Grand Faslairt, Royal Order of the Red Branch Eri.

He serves as a speaker for the Valley of Chicago Scottish Rite. He is the current Junior Deacon of the Illinois Lodge of Research and an Honorary Member of African Lodge no. 459 Prince Hall Affiliated. He holds memberships is the Masonic Society, the Scottish Rite Research Society S.J., the Phylaxis Society, the Philalethes Society, and the Quatuor Coronati Correspondence Circle.

Charles M. Harper Sr. is the author of the controversial book, Freemasonry in Black and White, found at www.freemasonryinblackandwhite.com as well as a monthly featured writer for the Living Stones Magazine found at www.livingstonesmagazine.com. He has appeared on the Whence Came You podcast found at www.wcypodcast.com, as well as the Roundtable Table Discussion Live found at: www.themasonicroundtable.com/2014/06/episode-17-clandestine-masonry/ on the topic of Clandestine Freemasonry. Charles Harper's introduction Video on his book is available at M.A.T.S.O.L., Masonic Awareness at the Speed of Light, found at: www.matsol.info/index.php/weofm-videos/video/freemasonry-in-black-and-white-bro-charles-m-harper-sr as well as the *Lewis Masonic Video Library*. As this book is being written, the book *Freemasonry in Black and White* has inspired talks on a documentary on spurious Freemasonry and currently a show is in the works.

Charles M. Harper Sr. travels around the United States giving well received presentations on various culturally relative aspects of his book using moral philosophy found within masonic ritual. He delivers an insight on his experiences having held memberships in both the dark world of clandestine Freemasonry, and his journey to becoming a traditional Freemason, the cultural impact experienced, both positive and negative expressed by both ethnic groups, Black and White, which historically dominates the Masonic landscape of the United States.

More information on the book Freemasonry in Black and White, previous reviews and upcoming presentations can be found at: www.freemasonryinblackandwhite.com

Bibliography

[i] Clandestine (2007) Penguin English Dictionary. London: Penguin
[ii] Mackey, A. (1873) Encyclopedia of Freemasonry, London, New York
[iii] Jones, B. (1950) Freemasons' Guide and Compendium, Great Britain
[iv] Jones, B.
[v] Jones, B.
[vi] Grand Lodge of Pennsylvania Proceedings February 3, 1783
[vii] Belton, J. (2012) The English Masonic union of 1813: A Tale Antient and Modern, United Kingdom
[viii] SHORT TALK BULLETIN - Vol. XIII December, 1935 No.12
[ix] Burgess, R., Croteau, J., Foulds, A., Newell, A., Roach, Jr., J., Swanson, C. (2013) a Sublime Brotherhood: Two Hundred Years of Scottish Rite Freemasonry in the Northern Masonic Jurisdiction, Lexington, Ma.
[x] Regular (2011) The American Heritage(r) Dictionary of the English Language, Boston
[xi] www.conferenceofgrandmasterspha.org/gjlinks.asp
[xii] Conference of Grand Masters of North America, 1952
[xiii] www.thephylaxis.org/bogus/regularity.php
[xiv] United Grand Lodge of England Basic Principles for Grand Lodge Recognition;
Accepted by the Grand Lodge, September 4, 1929
[xv] www.recognitioncommission.org
[xvi] Mackey, A.
[xvii] Grand Lodge of Louisiana, February 1869
[xviii] www.tmwsolgl.org
[xix] Prince Hall Masonic Journal (Fall 2012) Official Publication of the Most Worshipful Prince Hall Grand Lodge of Illinois.
[xx] Lilly, D.A. (2014) "We are NOT all Brothers: An Introduction into Clandestine Freemasonry."
[xxi] Women's Lodges in the USA
Chartered by the Women's Grand Lodge of Belgium, History of Woman's Freemasonry.
[xxii] United Grand Lodge of England, March 10, 1999 Quarterly Communication
[xxiii] Tabbert, M. (2006) American Freemasons: Three Centuries of Building Communities, National Heritage Museum
[xxiv] Masonicinfo.com
[xxv] Phylaxis Society

[xxvi] www.facebook.com/MasonicOrder/photos/a.182446978436500.48206.140919472589251/718259318188594/?type=3&theater

[xxvii] THE MASONIC HIGH COUNCIL THE MOTHER HIGH COUNCIL ANCIENT AND HONOURABLE FRATERNITY OF FREE AND ACCEPTED MASONS, www.rgle.org.uk

[xxviii] RA H Morrow, Grand Secretary, 2005, COMMS/RAHM/JMI-l/sdh/Gsecsl, United Grand Lodge of England

[xxix] International Free and Accepted Modern Masons History, www.internationalmasons.org/our_history.html

[xxx] www.internationalmasons.org

[xxxi] The Grand Chapter of Royal Arch Masons of the State of Illinois, www.illinoisyorkrite.org

[xxxii] www.aeaonms.org/PDF%20Documents/antihazingpolicy.pdf

[xxxiii] www.internationalmasons.org/departments/imperial_council.html

[xxxiv] Walkes Jr., J. (1974) Phylaxis magazine, Volume 1, Number 1.

[xxxv] Short Talk Bulletin - Dec. 1935, Masonic Service Association of North America

[xxxvi] Discrimination. (2001). In World of sociology, The Gale Group.

[xxxvii] www.nytimes.com/2009/07/03/us/03masons.html?_r=0

[xxxviii] www.masonic-crusade.com/gallery/1/Expulsion%20Edict.pdf

[xxxix] www.masonic-crusade.com/wordpress/

[xl] Grand Master's Agenda 142nd Annual Communication Most Worshipful Grand Lodge A.F & A.M. of the State of West Virginia, Wheeling, West Virginia. October 9 & 10, 2006.

[xli] Grand Master of the Masonic Grand Lodge of New South Wales and Australian Capital Territory edict concerning esoteric studies in the Masonic Fraternity given at the Grand Communication June 13, 2012 which includes points 1-7.

[xlii] www.thetruthaboutdangannon.weebly.com

[xliii] Webb, T. (1797) Freemason's Monitor, Published by C. Moore at the Masonic Review Office in 1865.

[xliv] Jandt, F. (2013) an Introduction to Intercultural Communication: Identities in a Global Community.

[xlv] The Restoration of Amity between the United Grand Lodge of England and the Most Worshipful Prince Hall Grand Lodge of Massachusetts. April 12, 2007

[xlvi] Prince Hall Grand Lodge of Massachusetts sent a letter to the United Grand Lodge of England in 1988

www.ingramcontent.com/pod-product-compliance
Lightning Source LLC
Chambersburg PA
CBHW030416100426
42812CB00028B/2989/J